SUNNY

Born Anuradha C. in Trichy to lawyer-businessman Chandra and his wife Githamani, Anu Hasan grew up climbing mango trees, playing street cricket, and watching *The Sound of Music* seventeen times. She called herself Anuradha C. for the longest time in an attempt to seek anonymity, until she finally gave up and acknowledged that she was one of the Hasans. In a media career spanning six languages and two countries, she hosted Tamil Nadu's most successful celebrity talk show to date (*Koffee with Anu*), presented her cookery show *En Samaiyal Araiyil* as chef, hosted reality and game shows and acted in Tamil, Telugu, Malayalam, English and Arabic movies (she played the lead role in the movie *Indira*) among other things. Actor, businesswoman, writer, singer, company director, CEO and entrepreneur, Anu heads South India Cine Creations and is a director in an IT company dealing in enterprise mobility solutions. She lives in the UK but shuttles between India and the UK on work. *Sunny Side Up* is Anu Hasan's first book.

SUNNY SIDE UP

ANU HASAN

Collins

First published in India in 2014 by Collins
An imprint of HarperCollins *Publishers*

P-ISBN: 978-93-5136-386-6
E-ISBN: 978-93-5136-387-3

2 4 6 8 10 9 7 5 3 1

HarperCollins *Publishers*
A-75, Sector 57, Noida, Uttar Pradesh 201301, India
77-85 Fulham Palace Road, London W6 8JB, United Kingdom
Hazelton Lanes, 55 Avenue Road, Suite 2900, Toronto, Ontario M5R
3L2 and 1995 Markham Road, Scarborough, Ontario M1B 5M8, Canada
25 Ryde Road, Pymble, Sydney, NSW 2073, Australia
195 Broadway, New York, NY 10007, USA

Typeset in 11/14.5 Linux Libertine by
R. Ajith Kumar

Printed and bound at
Thomson Press (India) Ltd

To my parents:

Amma and Appa, my champions, my wings
You gave me more than just material things
You are the best I could have ever wanted
You stood by this child undaunted
Amma and Appa, my champions, my wings

CONTENTS

INTRODUCTION

People often tell me, 'You are such a positive and happy person,' and it always makes me think, Hah! I am such a good actor.

I think they are probably right, most of the time anyway. I can be quite irrational and melodramatic when I get depressed but thankfully those moments do not last long.

It was my husband who got me started on the idea for the book. I had been writing a column for *Just For Women (JFW)* for the last six years when Graham said, 'Why don't you use some of the content to write a book?' Around the same time, I met a dear friend and publisher extraordinaire, Gandhi Kannadhasan, who recommended that I get in touch with Priya Doraswamy, a literary agent. Priya and I spoke several times and after many phone and email exchanges, we agreed to work together. Priya suggested I write something in the self-help genre. Melding Graham's and Priya's ideas, I found myself writing, and in the process realized that something wonderful was happening. I was able to look at my own life objectively. As Kahlil Gibran said, 'The mountain to the climber is clearer from the plains.'

By writing this book, I have been able to refocus my attention on the rare moments of clarity that I seem to have had when I was challenged with difficulties. I have looked back on my life with kinder eyes, I have laughed again at the experiences that were funny, felt sad for the things that knocked me down and happy that I emerged feeling quietly satisfied about having done the best I could at every stage of my life.

I have also had the opportunity to acknowledge all the people who have made me the person I am. And if that isn't self-help, I don't know what is.

This book chronicles, mainly for your amusement and hopefully for a teeny bit of inspiration, incidents from my life. My idiosyncrasies might make you smile or even strike a chord somewhere. I hope reading this gives you as much reason to smile as there is when life is sunny side up!

Anu Hasan
December 2014

FRIENDS

I choose to start with this chapter because I cannot emphasize the importance of friends enough. Although I am the kind of person who doesn't like to depend on other people to the extent possible, I have depended on my friends at every point in my life when my confidence has been shaken. And my faith in them has never been proved wrong.

At any given point in my life there are always about six people who are very close to me. The first thing that strikes me is that only four form my core. Kripa – my friend from college – my soulmate and blindly loyal supporter. Everyone needs one of those. The one friend who will stand by you even when you make mistakes. The one who will be there to help you get up despite the fact that you stubbornly ignored their words of caution and fell on your face. And, most importantly, the one who will never ever say 'I told you so' – that's Kripa.

The next is Ranga – I'm probably the only one who calls him that. Ranga is someone whom I have never seen flustered. He too has been my friend from my college days. If Kripa is my support, Ranga is my reality check. He is quick to pull me back from my melodramatic moments and make me see the funnier side of things.

Then there is Abe – the rational practical thinker I turn to for analysis and hypothesis. He never tells me whether I am right or wrong. He merely allows me to think things through, asking appropriate questions along the way. (After that we go out to dinner and eat more than we should!)

And finally there is Purni – the special educationist whom I have known for a few years now. She is the one with whom I can talk for hours about philosophy, nonsense, problems and complaints. We share this equally and although neither offers a solution, we both feel better having each other to vent.

> **Note to self:**
> Quality is always better than quantity, especially when it comes to friends. Having a few good friends beats being Ms Popularity hands down.

So there you go, my four pillars – support, reality check, analysis and vent. Brilliant combination, really.

And then there is Kutty. This is the name I have given Aparna Pillai – it wouldn't take a genius to guess why – she stands at five feet and a bit and I stand a good eight inches taller.

She is quite a character. Although I have been her sounding board and the big sister who generously doles out advice, she plays a rather sweet role in my life.

A few years ago, when I received a call from the German Consulate, I was curious. When I realized the call was regarding an invitation to The Berlinale, I was cautiously excited. Excited because it was flattering to receive such an invitation and to the Berlin Film Festival at that, cautious because I was not sure I deserved it.

When I mentioned my misgivings to them, I was assured that in their eyes I was a suitable candidate, which quashed my reservations at once. Still I dilly-dallied, not entirely sure whether I should go, using various reasons including the cold, inability to fly economy (oooh, diva!), etc, etc. Every one of them got shot down by the people who were coordinating the arrangements and suddenly it was Monday and I had to leave for Berlin on Wednesday.

Two days to get everything in order, finish shoots, meet deadlines ... it was enough to drive a sane person crazy. But I never claimed to be completely sane, did I?

I was editing and dubbing till 6 p.m. on the day I was to take the flight out. I still needed to pack and a number of things had to be bought. I always knew I was good at multitasking but that day I proved myself to be a multitasker above par. I had a business meeting sandwiched between editing and I still managed to call Kutty to say goodbye as I drove to the dubbing theatre.

Kutty is one of those people whose constant effort has been to make me look a little more put together than I usually am. She has had limited success so far. Her first question was: 'What are you going to wear in Berlin, Big A?' (We have the same initials, she is Kutty and I am Big – get it?) I glossed over the details and her antenna immediately picked up the signals. She cut through the bull and asked me to describe the clothes I was taking. I fumbled for a bit and then sheepishly admitted that I hadn't packed yet and therefore hadn't thought about it.

Naturally she was aghast. 'How can you go to the Berlin

Film Festival and not have planned your wardrobe?' she asked.

I laughed weakly and replied that the less put together I looked, the greater the chances of people thinking I was a mad genius. She wasn't amused.

'What about winter clothes?' she asked impatiently.

I replied that Kripa had sent me her muffler, a long black coat and gloves and I would manage with those.

'For ten days?' she asked, her voice dripping disbelief.

I hummed and hawed and hastily added that another friend was on standby with a few coats and that in any case I was going to raid my cousin's wardrobe.

'And when were you planning on doing that?' she asked.

'After I finish editing and dubbing,' I replied in my most convincing voice.

She sighed and said, 'I'll get some stuff for you and come over.'

The long suffering tone would have bothered me if I wasn't certain it was an indulgent one. Ignoring my feeble protests, Kutty set out on her mission.

After racing to meet my deadlines on various projects, I was fatigued and ready to curl up and go to sleep. At 9 p.m. she breezed into my house, a princess on the warpath. Her nephew plonked himself on the modha looking like he was getting ready to watch a comedy. She ordered her driver to drop the huge bundle of winter clothes she had pulled out of her wardrobe. She was hauling two shopping bags.

For a pint-sized creature she sure knew how to command instant obedience. She ordered me to try on the new clothes she had bought for me in case I had to go for a diplomatic dinner. Then she made me try them on again with thermal wear inside. When she waved the fifth outfit under my nose I belligerently told her I wasn't going to try on any more clothes.

She sniffed in disdain and proceeded to poke around the things I had accumulated on my living room floor. 'You can't possibly wear a white shirt with black pants! You'll look like a waiter!' 'Don't you dare combine this shoe with that outfit!' 'Do you have a handbag? You can't go for a diplomatic dinner with a wallet!' 'Is this shoe going to last the winter?'

'That's a Nike!' I said indignantly.

'Yeah and the toe is peeling off.'

I scratched my head, wondering how to convince her that it was perfectly wearable. I caught her nephew's eye and the grin on his face was a clear indication that I was losing. I grinned back at him and quietly gave in to her. She was, after all, the expert.

She sorted through the combinations I was supposed to wear, discarding and adding to what was turning into an alarmingly large pile of clothes. I could hear my mother's voice in my head – 'Oru kutty tripp ukku so much luggage?' (So much luggage for a small trip?) But I forgot, this was a 'kutty' overseas trip – a different ballgame altogether.

After running her critical eye over the pile of clothes and accessories, she delved into the contents of my make-up kit. 'Too pink!' 'So not in!' – she quickly segregated things. Wanting to contribute, I timidly held up an eye pencil which got rejected for being 'too obvious'. Finally she leaned back and pronounced me a fit candidate for European eyes.

I heaved a sigh of relief and was about to declare that I was now ready to sleep, when I saw the fatigue on her face. With a surge of guilt I realized that she had had a long and tiring day herself and had still come charging to my rescue.

I thanked her with a hug and she brushed it aside. She swept out again, throwing a threat over her shoulder about how I'd BETTER wear the right combinations. I smiled at her pretended brusqueness – for under all that was a loving, generous person who could sniff a fashion disaster a mile away. And I am never too far off from being one.

As I crawled into bed to snatch a few hours of sleep before my flight to Berlin, I thought how lucky I was to have friends who ride in to my rescue. I've never understood why Kutty took me up as a case for reform but I am glad she did. While I am happy being as dishevelled as I normally am, there is indeed a pleasure in being well turned out.

> **Note to self:** It is as important to receive gracefully as it is to give unstintingly.

For Kutty, I am a never-ending project. Ah well, you don't hear ME objecting!

So there you go. Friend #5 accounted for. I don't know who #6 is, perhaps it is a position occupied by different people at different times... Or perhaps it belongs to Jacob, an unfinished chapter in my life. Or a chapter that finished too soon.

I remember him in the most unexpected of moments. I recall once I was driving along quite happily when the radio station started to play Michael Learns To Rock. With a swiftness born from painful memories, I switched off the radio. But not before my mind shot to thoughts of Jacob. Tough, sweet Jacob with whom I had spent many happy yet intense moments in college. He was one of those guys who pretended to be tough and sneered at the guys who spoke to girls. He would walk around with a swagger, his collar turned up. He had such a reluctant smile. He would press his lips together and grit his teeth almost as if he was doing his best to hold back a full-throated guffaw, but invariably a smile escaped.

I remember his denim jacket – the one that was a bit too short for him. I remember him, along with the other guys on my backstage team, picking me up and throwing me into the pond. I remember two years of fun and two years of anger.

It seems so silly, when I think about it now. I was the coordinator for the Department of Backstage, the first female co-ord in a male-dominated department. I was there to prove a point. And prove it I would, even if it meant I broke my back trying to haul as many wooden cots as a guy could. The flat surfaces of the cots would act as beds when we wanted to sleep; they could be turned to face the audience and when placed one beside the other, the cots became a wall. When piled one on top of the other we had the first floor. I would work along side the guys, building the set on the stage, hammering away with a ferocity that came from who knows where. Jacob was one of the guys on my team and one day I overheard him say something which at that time seemed extremely chauvinistic. In fact I don't even remember what it was. But I was so incensed that I stopped talking to him.

I cold-shouldered him for the better part of two years,

starting off with an anger I never meant to last. I don't think he knew why I was angry for a long time. And when he did, he retaliated with an indifference he never meant for a moment. But we had scripted our behaviour and as we continued down the paths we had forged, the gap between us widened. How young and stupid we were. Out of sheer pride, I refused to mend bridges and Jacob wasn't about to be outdone in the ego department either. For two years we carried on in this way.

It must have been extremely uncomfortable for our friends. We had common friends whom we hung out with frequently. And during those times we would laugh and talk to everyone except each other. Our friends saw this but knew better than to interfere in a war in which they would end up being collateral damage.

I don't know which one of our friends got sick of it but we were made to sit down and talk to each other. It was almost towards the end of my time in college, the last month, I think. I remember feeling very sad and very silly. After an uncomfortable start, both of us decided to bury the non-existent hatchet. I wonder what happened to the conciliatory painting I made for him. Maybe it lies in some dusty attic. Maybe he threw it away with all his college stuff.

> **Note to self:** If you care enough to get angry with a friend, care enough to make up – quickly.

We didn't get too much time together after that. The final exams started and with both of us struggling to catch up after a whole year spent doing everything but attend classes, we hardly had time to rebuild our friendship.

When that semester ended, we all travelled back to Madras in the same train and later I even spent a few days hanging out at Elliot's beach with him and a few other guys Slowly, as my life took me on my own path of colourful mistakes, his took him to the Middle East, and we lost touch. Almost two years went by without us meeting or even writing to each other.

I think we even forgot each other.

I remember the day with painful clarity. I was driving along listening to Michael Learns To Rock, when a mutual friend of ours called me.

I flew down to Bangalore for Jacob's funeral. He had died in a bike accident in the Middle East. I stared at the face I thought I knew so well. In my mind's eye I could still see that smile of his. But the face I saw in the coffin bore no resemblance to the handsome young man I had known.

In some ways, I am glad that I couldn't recognize him that day. That way, my memory of him continues to be of him in his too-short denim jacket with the collar turned up, smiling at me reluctantly as he raked his hair back. I wish we had not fought and I wish we had not allowed our friendship to go adrift.

It has been more than fifteen years, yet I take the coward's way out and try not to think about Jacob. And when some radio channel inadvertently plays Michael Learns To Rock, I turn it off, not because I want to forget Jacob, but because I don't want to remember his absence.

But I think it is time I stopped

> **Note to self:** I have to admit – even in the face of death – that life goes on.

pretending and I think it is time I acknowledged the fact that I miss Jacob.

So from a friend who is no longer there, I move on to the next category of friends.

Sometimes you just need to get out and enjoy yourself. I have a group of friends I can do that with.

Maybe I reserve that sixth spot for this kind of friend.

One day I got a call from my production manager who told me that owing to some problem with dates, the next day's shoot had been cancelled. I was thrilled. It was like someone telling me there's no school today. While I love my work, an unexpected holiday, you must admit, is delightful. My mind was whirling with a list of all the things I could do the next day. I texted a friend of mine asking him if he would like to go canoeing in Mudaliarkuppam. He agreed immediately, saying he needed a break and would take time off from work. Not satisfied with corrupting one young soul, I targeted another friend. My SMS to him read: *I am texting you to urge you to bunk work for half a day tomorrow so we can go canoeing. Can can? Canoeing?*

Within minutes he called me. 'Gosh, what a good influence you are! Where is this place?'

'On ECR, it won't take us more than an hour to get there. We should leave around two or so, so that it isn't too hot by the time we reach. We can even ride the water scooters.'

'Aha! Why half a day? For that I am willing to call in sick the whole day!' he replied.

'You are in office and you just made an incriminating statement and your dad is going to catch you out,' I teased him. (He worked with his dad, you see!)

'No, no. The moment I saw your text, I logged off my computer and ran out to the teashop to call you.'

'Super,' I said in glee. 'So fall sick tomorrow. I will pick you up and the three of us can go.'

I spent the rest of the evening grinning.

The next morning, I started organizing the food – that's my area of speciality, planning the menu for a picnic. I got Australian grapes, fruit yoghurt and apple juice. I made stuffed ham sandwiches and smoked chicken salad. Half the fun on these trips is the food.

We set off on the drive and reached Mudaliarkuppam at the perfect time. There were no tourists and we had the entire place to ourselves. Neither of my friends wanted to try the water scooter so I asked them to wait for me while I took it for a spin. I roared around in tight circles on the water and then zoomed off James Bond style into the backwaters. Catch a guy being content with watching a woman do such stuff! Both of them enthusiastically decided to give it a go and I must admit they were not too bad for boys.

Then came the canoeing. We took a canoe each and started rowing. I took my food with me, they took their cigarettes. We all have our priorities.

I rowed nonstop for about twenty minutes and made measly progress, but hey, who said I was contending in the Olympics? As with everything in my life, once I was satisfied with the progress I had made, I leaned back and decided to take it easy for a while. I stretched out on the canoe and stared lazily at the evening sky. I floated around for how long I do not know when I heard my friend say, 'Dei! Anaadha ponam da!' For those who don't speak Tamil, this phrase is the equivalent of 'unclaimed body'. I laughed and almost fell out of the canoe and exacted my revenge for that irreverent remark by sitting up and proceeding to eat my sandwich accompanied by appropriate noises of delight. By the time I attacked the mango yoghurt they were both wearing sufficiently satisfying looks of yearning. So I took pity on them and gave them the yoghurt, which was disgustingly sweet anyway.

A fat drop of rain reminded us that we had an hour's drive ahead of us so we rowed back and clambered onto the dock. After cheerfully waving goodbye to the Tamil Nadu Tourism Development Corporation employees who run the place and giving them the two remaining cups of mango yoghurt) we set off for the drive back home.

'I am so glad we managed to do this,' I sighed in satisfaction.

The one who had pretended to fall sick said, 'You made me bunk work but I forgive you.'

I looked at him with mock innocence and said, 'What do you mean? I did no such thing.'

He waved his phone at me. 'I have evidence.' Darn guy had saved the text I had sent him. I sweetly asked him if I could see it. He just as sweetly refused to give me the phone.

> **Note to self:** It is important to have a friend you can have a good time with. Nothing more – nothing less

Later he sent me a text: *I am glad I came on the trip, Anu akka. I really enjoyed it.*

I saved that message.

When I extend the circle of friends more people come to mind, those who are both friends and mentors. There are many, but one couple will always have a special place in my heart – Visu mama and Leela mami. They are both well into their seventies, perhaps even early eighties. I met them at the YMCA years ago and have continued to stay in touch with them.

When I tell them about some of the things people do to irk me at the YMCA, they smile and say, 'Forget them, Anu. Silly people abound in this world. Did you have a good run today?' And I smile at how quickly they manage to remind me to push away the things that don't matter lest I lose focus on my purpose for being at the YMCA in the first place.

I don't know what it is about them but to me they signify everything that a human being who has lived seventy-odd years should have: love, acceptance, wisdom and, most importantly, the ability to give all this without expecting anything in return.

I marvel at their ability to give that which is so precious and rare. In my experience, I've found that some people are your friends mostly because of who you are in the world and not who you are inside. While I have some really genuine friends, I am always careful when I admit new acquaintances into my inner circle. This caution has served me well but it doesn't stop me from marvelling at and instantly allowing beautiful people like this couple into my world. These are the kind of people whose very presence chips away at my cynical approach to life. Their gentle smile mocks at my caution,

Note to self: It is important to cut out external noise when focusing on the things that matter, lest they detract from the simple pleasures in life.)

their wisdom makes me wish time would go faster so I too might learn what they have. But the most beautiful of all is their acceptance of who I am, which humbles me.

PARENTS

To have friends is one thing but to be blessed with great parents is the luck of the draw. You know what they say – you choose your friends, not your family. But when it comes to my parents, I couldn't have chosen better had I been given a choice. Although I must confess, I did not always feel this way.

I too went through a phase where I thought my parents didn't understand me, that their disapproval of me was unwarranted. You know, the usual resentful teenage phase (which continued until I was almost thirty-five but that's another story). However, my childhood was both normal as well as more colourful than most.

If I did something wrong I got a spanking. This happened quite frequently. Every instance was justified except for one occasion. I was playing hide and seek and my friend who couldn't find me, went and told my mum that she thought I was trapped inside a building under construction. My friend got her part of the story wrong, but my mother panicked and when she found me right outside the house, she didn't ask me where I had been hiding. She dragged me home and spanked me for having put myself in danger.

When it came to spanking, both my brother and I used to get our fair share, though I was the more melodramatic recipient. I would yell and bawl and beg for forgiveness and swear never to do it again. My brother was quieter. Once I noticed that I got spanked for longer than he did and I thought the secret to this was the blank non-reactive looks he gave my mother when he was being spanked. I decided to try it out the next time and ended up infuriating my mother even more. 'Pretending to be like Nirmal, are you?' she said and spanked me a few more times. So I went back to bawling and pleading piteously while running around the dining table trying to escape.

> **Note to self:** There is no blueprint one can follow to extricate oneself from trouble. Find out what works for you and stick to it.

When I discovered that my mother was loathe to climb stairs I finally found a way to escape being spanked. I would run a few circles around the dining table and then run up the stairs and stand on the landing and swear never to do it again. Needless to say, I spent quite some time on that landing.

Those punishments didn't do me any harm. I do not harbour any sympathy for the little devil that I was. And I certainly do not think that my more than robust psyche was damaged or bruised because of the punishment meted out to me.

I was a curious child and much given to flights of fancy. Therefore I was quite the little liar. My father has always been adept at catching me out when I lie, so it was my mum who became the lucky recipient of my tall tales. The earliest

incident I can remember is from the time when I was about
six years old. I came home from school one day and told my
mother, 'Amma, there was quicksand in the school and two
girls nearly fell in. I saved them, so to congratulate me they
called me in front of everyone during morning assembly and
gave me *cholam*.' My mother, to her credit, believed only half
of it – that I had saved some kids and was congratulated for
my brave deed. She thought I didn't know the meaning of
quicksand and was using it to refer to a slippery spot on the
ground. She should have known better, considering I was
reading Alistair Maclean and Jack Higgins by then.

When my dad came home that evening, my proud mother
narrated the story to him. His reaction was: 'Really? Is that
true? Radha, come here...' The moment I heard the chiding
note in his voice, I blubbered and stammered that I had been
lying all this while. My mother was very upset – not because
I had lied but because she had believed me, a six year old.
To this day she hasn't forgiven me for this.

But that didn't stop me from making other attempts. But
even now, after all these years, I feel nervous when I have
to go against my father's wishes or lie to him to cover up.
I said nervous. Not unable. But mostly unsuccessful. I like
it that way. I think I might actually feel disappointed if my
dad did not catch me out on my lies. No matter how old I
get, I am still his little girl.

Despite being gullible, my mother was very clear about
the kind of person she wanted me to be. I was never told
I couldn't do something because I was a girl. I was told I
couldn't do something because it was WRONG. My parents
never thought my being a girl made me any less capable.

In fact I was given more responsibilities than my brother. And to a large extent that shaped me into the independent woman I am today.

As a child, I was always encouraged to be brave. My mother can be childishly afraid of things at times and incredibly brave at other times. I seem to have inherited more of her courage than her fears. A few years ago, when I was going through my divorce, Subha akka, who is a very close family friend, told me the story of the dog. One day, when I was about eight years old, a girl in my class was being nasty. When I stood up to her, she said, 'When you come visit Subha akka, I'll set my dog on you.' So that weekend when I was visiting, I asked akka to accompany me to the girl's house, which was just a few hundred yards away. When we reached the gate, I asked her to stand outside. I went in, rang the bell and when the door opened and the girl came out, I said, 'Where is your dog? Go on, let me see your dog.' The girl got very worried (probably that I would complain to her mother) and ran away. Akka says I stood at the door for a second, pulled it close behind me and slowly walked back to the gate and told akka, 'We can go now.'

I have no recollection of the incident but everyone in Subha akka's family seems to remember it. In fact they say it was an indication of the kind of person I was going to be. And they were right. For most of my life I faced my fears and perceived threats, but somewhere along the line I became more fearful than I had to be. Every time there was a situation, I didn't want to handle it because I was afraid. And because I wasn't handling it, my imagination came up with various possible outcomes. The mornings began with an intense feeling of dread. And it was only when I was reminded of the story of the dog that I realized I had forgotten as an adult what I once knew as a child. I felt sheepish and began to handle problems again instead of hiding from them. It was tough but I felt better doing that instead of imagining the many awful outcomes as a result of handling it the wrong way.

That was a very useful lesson to learn. If something scares me I stop, turn around and face it – because I know that I will find it more frightening if I were to run away.

My mother's style of child-rearing, while effective, was not unusual in India. But my father's style has always made me marvel at his wisdom. He has never to this day raised his voice at me. There was something about him that commanded instant respect and obedience. If my mother taught me right and wrong, how to take care of myself and how to be brave, my father was the one with forethought and planning. He looked many years ahead and set rules that would help us later in life.

> **Note to self:** Never run from your fears. The moment you turn your back on them, your imagination makes them worse than they actually are.

Consider this rule: You cannot say, 'I will not eat this because I do not like it.' You will finish what is on your plate. If you like something you can have a second helping.

This lowered my threshold of acceptance when it came to food. I appreciate good food but if I have to get by on badly made food, I still consider it fuel and keep going. I know of friends who gave up the opportunity to study in a great university or live in another country just because they could not bear eating the food. When I told my father this, he smiled in that gentle, infinitely wise way of his and said, 'Why do you think I said that when you were a child?'

The other thing he did was to train my brother and me to eat meat. Coming from a Brahmin family, meat was taboo and we have never brought non-vegetarian food into my parents' house. But as children we used to go out for dinner every other week and eat non-vegetarian food. My mother, who was vegetarian, was a sport and sat at the same table to eat her boring vegetarian fare. Appa tells me he did this to help us survive in any country. At a time when vegetarianism was not as common as it is today, being non-vegetarian was definitely an advantage.

> **Note to self:** Do not underestimate the influence of seemingly unimportant childhood lessons.

But the most invaluable lesson Appa taught me was when I was at BITS Pilani. I have spoken about this in many interviews but I can never stress the importance of this lesson enough. I entered BITS Pilani with the unshakeable belief that I was a genius. Of course, I was also more interested in the fibreglass basketball boards and 3-pointers, but since I was convinced of my genius, I was certain I could effortlessly score good marks. Surely someone who consistently obtained one of the top three ranks in class with no great effort and scored 193 out of 200 in physics after playing cricket on the streets for three of the four study holidays had to be a genius! I was wrong, obviously, but I didn't realize that until the end of the term, after I had done everything except attend class.

As a result I was in real danger of not clearing the semester. It was a very rude shock to an arrogant teenager. And so what did I do? I called home and cried.

My mum was not very sympathetic. She said, 'If you come home, you will have to sit in the kitchen and wash dishes – is that what you want to do? Talk to your dad.' And my father the wonderful philosopher came on the phone. He listened to my story which was punctuated with loud hiccups and sniffs and then asked me quietly, 'Why do you think I sent you to BITS Pilani?'

I replied in a small voice, 'To study, pa.'

He responded calmly, 'No, I sent you to Pilani to learn about life. And I think you have just learnt your first lesson.' And that was the end of the conversation. When I realized no one was going to give me an easy way out, I worked very hard to clear my courses for the year.

After that kind of beginning, it was a steady uphill task to graduate with the grades I made. But I did it and that is something I look back on with a sense of achievement.

My father, who has been my constant unwavering support – does he know how much I count on him being there for me in his inimitable non-intrusive style? Does he know how secure and safe he has always made me feel, even when I faced the repercussions of some of the worst decisions in my life? Maybe it is time to tell him.

> **Note to self:** I make my decisions and I face the consequences. That's life.

But it wasn't just serious lessons that I learnt from my parents. My mother imbibed in me her love for life. Small things make her happy. She can see a pretty flower and feel excited that she had the opportunity to see it. She gets thrilled when she finds an unexpected cup of coffee and hot samosas. She is blunt, open and sometimes tactless but has a heart of gold and an ability to see the funny side of things.

The odd thing about Amma is that although she loves visiting new places and exploring, when it comes to technology she always backs away. I couldn't even get her to learn how to send text messages. Not that she cannot do it, she will not learn. Funny mummy!

The advent of mobile phones has made such a difference to our lives. The good thing about cell phones is that you have everyone's number stored. The bad thing about cell-phones is that you have everyone's number stored. There were days when I used to know phone numbers like the back of my hand, but no longer. Except for a few, I don't even bother trying to remember people's phone numbers. Now this poses a problem when I lose my device and, consequently, all the numbers in the phonebook. People who speak to me on a regular basis are miffed when I timidly ask, 'Ummm ... who is this please?' When I tell them I've lost my phone there is a note of disbelief in their response. It's a good thing I lose my phone only once every eight or ten months.

My mother told me a hilarious story. She had gone to visit the doctor and they asked her for a telephone number they could reach her at when the reports were ready. Unhesitatingly she rattled off a number, not realizing that the phone number she had given was the neighbour's. She got out of the hospital and decided to call the maid to give her some instructions. So she called the number she had just given at the hospital and found it busy. Her overactive imagination (which I have inherited) got into gear and she thought the darn maid must be making long-distance calls. She cancelled her other plans and decided to go home to catch the maid red-handed.

When she reached home the maid said the phone had not been used the entire morning. My mother gave her cell phone to the driver, called out the same number and asked him to dial. The driver obliged and the phone rang – at my neighbour's. He told my mother it was ringing. But the phone didn't ring inside the house. My mother was about to ask him to disconnect when my neighbour answered the phone. The driver quickly disconnected and told my mother, 'Amma, how come some lady is picking up your phone? Do you think the telephone exchange has given your number to someone else?' My mother replied indignantly, 'What nonsense! I shall complain to the telephone exchange! I have had this number for the past thirty years. Call the number again and ask who it is!'

The driver called back and my neighbour picked up.

The driver asked, 'Who is this?'

'This is CC mami.'

'Oh, hello, mami! How come you are answering our land line?'

'But this is my phone.'

The driver relayed this information to my mother and it suddenly dawned on her. She took the phone from the driver and told CC mami, 'Mami, I went to the doctor and they asked me for a number and I gave them your number by mistake. What a lot of confusion! So if they call from the doctor's to tell you that the reports are ready, don't worry, they are talking about my reports.'

I thought the story ended there, but there was more. CC mami replied, 'It is all right, Githa, I will give them your number. Oh, and by the way, if the architect calls you to ask when he has to come to submit the drawings, give him my number, will you?'

Incidents like this abound. I too have been on the receiving end of her overactive imagination. It happened when I was at a birthday party. It was late in the night. I wasn't particularly enjoying myself but it was an obligation so I was hanging round disinterestedly, waiting for them to cut the cake so I could make my escape. I had my phone in the back pocket of my jeans and as I leaned against the wall, I hit the speed dial for my mother by mistake.

I can see how it must have appeared. It's nearly midnight and your daughter calls you – your first reaction is worry, even panic. My mother answered and since the phone was still in my back pocket, naturally I couldn't hear her. But she could hear noises in the background. She probably said hello a few times and then disconnected.

Moments later, I idly pulled out my phone from my pocket and realized what had happened. So I called her back and guess what she said: 'Oh, I am so glad you are okay. I thought you had been kidnapped and you were calling me and leaving the phone on so I could guess where you were and try and rescue you.' I thought she was joking. When I realized she meant it, I burst out laughing. Thankfully she joined me. Over the years I have come to understand two things – my imagination and my ability to laugh at the funny things in life come from my mother. But for a woman who appears to be so light-hearted and simple, my mother exhibits a core of steel which I think surprises even her.

Case in point, her diagnosis of breast cancer. I was in Madras at that time and my father was travelling. My mother was alone in Trichy. The doctor advised her to undergo mastectomy and asked her if she would like to check with her family. My mother, who is afraid to cross the road by herself, who cringes from picking up the mobile if it is an unknown number and who generally displays all signs of helplessness, responded, 'I don't have to ask them. It is my body, my decision.' And so she started a journey that would have been frightening for many people, and she did so with a courage that I never cease to marvel at. It was not an easy journey but she emerged from it with the same *joie de vivre* that she had before and it is this trait of her that makes me most proud.

I know that I, as a result of my genes as well as my life choice (no kids), am at a high risk for breast cancer. And I hope I will be as brave as my mother if and when I am faced with the same situation.

> **Note to self:** Fear is only one facet of a personality in one situation.

FAMILY

Over the years I have lost touch with everyone except immediate members of my family for various reasons (thankfully animosity isn't one of them). So when there is an invitation to, say, a *sashtyabdhipoorthi*, I sometimes set aside my usual reluctance to dress up and decide to go along with my parents simply because these family occasions are a riot. You meet your grandaunt's cousin's son-in-law and he greets you like a long-lost sibling. There is a kind of total acceptance.

But these occasions also make me feel like I am navigating through unchartered waters. I know they are family but I am usually hazy about how exactly we are related. Once I agreed to accompany my parents for one such occasion. What tipped the scale was that Jayam athai and Ammaayi athai were going to be there. They are my father's cousins and possess a wicked sense of humour. Although I haven't met them with any mentionable degree of frequency, they always greet me with affection. Jayam athai speaks her mind with an impish candour that makes it hard for you to feel offended, and Ammaayi athai does the same thing in a more subdued manner. They both possess the added nonchalance that comes with age and I thoroughly enjoy watching them.

The hall was filled with familiar faces and we were greeted with great excitement. My mother was hugged by various women and I had my cheeks pinched and my back patted – thumped, actually – with gusto. I couldn't stop grinning. Not for the first time I realized what it was to be bound by a common thread. The underlying subtext in every conversation was: 'You are family therefore I accept you.'

I looked around for my favourite people and found one of them. Jayam athai is a little bundle of energy. She bounded up to me and hugged me tight. Someone mentioned my TV show and she brushed aside the comment and said, 'I don't care what she does, she is my girl and I am happy to see her.' And then she shot me a grin to negate part of her statement. (Hopefully the first part but you never know with Jayam athai.)

I grinned back at her. She pulled me aside and said, 'Come and sit down. Want coffee?' and then promptly forgot about it and continued talking to my mother while maintaining her grip on my hand. I was happy to stand by her and listen to her chatter.

Ammaayi athai sailed in a little later. She is a regal lady and I love the way she exudes class. While Jayam athai is chirpy and confident and impish, Ammayi athai is elegant and confident with a droll sense of humour. When she too hugged me, my visit was complete. I had met both aunts. The fact that I was reintroduced (for the nth time) to the rest of the family was an added bonus.

I glanced at my watch and realized it was time for me to leave. Ammaayi athai looked patently disbelieving when I told her I had to get back to work and Jayam athai asked, 'What? You are leaving? What is it that you have to do?'

I replied, 'I have to go, athai. I just came to say hello to the two of you and attend the function.'

Without a pause she replied, 'Okay, hello.'

I laughed and hugged her. It is precisely this attitude that I find so lovely. There was no false polite 'Thank you for coming' or barely hidden disapproval that I was leaving early or even relief that I was. Just acceptance laced with a teasing barb. As I bid both the athais and the others goodbye, I was surprised by the flash of regret I felt. It had been so comforting to be in the midst of unconditional affection. The fact that our meetings were few and far between only served to make them view me with less criticism than I deserved.

Now I had to go back to a world where competence was not always an advantage and sincerity not necessarily welcome.

I walked to the door and turned around to look at the bustling hall. A smile burst forth from deep within me and I sailed out into my world with the sure knowledge that my ship was capable of weathering any storm.

And even though Gibran wrote about the house, I extended it to include family.

> **Note to self:**
> Remember the quote from Kahlil Gibran's *The Prophet* – 'Your house shall be not an anchor but a mast.'

It has been three years since the *sashtyabdhipoorthi*. As I write this, I remember with regret that Ammayi athai is no more. When the transcience of life is underlined, does it make you value people more?

HONESTY

Honesty would be the simplest solution to most things in life but there are people who will say that being completely honest is not that much of a good thing. And I have to agree with them. The problem is, I have never been hundred per cent accurate about when to be completely honest, when I should lie by omission and when I should just lie. So, while it might be the simplest solution, it certainly isn't the simplest thing to do. Most of the time I end up being honest when it is not really an endearing quality nor an easy one, considering the repercussions I have to face. But I can live with it. Which is not to say that I have never lied... Hah! As if! But I have realized that I am not good at keeping track of my lies and they always come back and bite me! So I minimize lies as much as possible.

> **Note to self:** If you have a poor long-term memory, honesty is the best policy.

I have been told that I am very critical of myself. I disagree. I know my strengths and weaknesses. So if people think I am critical of myself, they must also think I am arrogant about my capabilities and they would be right.

There are things I do well enough and that's a fact. I don't see any reason why I should not accept this.

I remember an incident during a TV show I was filming for – *Anu Alavum Bhayam Illai*. One of the tasks for the participants was to stand on a high wall and swing across to another with a rope. I was the presenter for the show and my role was to explain the rules, encourage them to do it and console them when they failed while the camera captured it all.

One of the participants was particularly competitive – and not just towards the other contestants, for she turned around and asked me, 'Can *you* do it?'

I was startled. I knew I couldn't swing across the rope because my upper body strength was just a little short of pathetic. I said as much but by then all the participants wanted me to do it. I think they wanted to see me fail. Bring me down to their level.

I was caught between a rock and a hard place. I hesitated for a moment and then said, 'I am the anchor, not a contestant. So I really don't have to compete with you.' I felt a sense of relief go through my director, Mohan, who was watching the exchange. Then I spoiled it all by adding, 'My upper body strength isn't very good so I can't swing across. But I am willing to try.'

And much to the direction team's dismay, I did. And I failed. Twice. It's all on camera, every clumsy attempt. It embarrassed everyone, including me. But it was done. I shrugged it off and we went on to the next task. I knew I was a good enough presenter that failing in one of the contestant's tasks wouldn't affect my credibility. I also believed that in showing them my weakness, I was also showing them my ability to accept it and move on and do my best with the job I was actually contracted to do. I have enough positive feedback on the way I presented the show to know that I succeeded in doing that.

And since we are talking about being honest, I knew I was a better presenter than any of the contestants (they too were actors and presenters). I also knew that my experience in stunt work and martial art meant I was just that little bit better at enacting fight sequences, bike and car chases than the participants, who were about fifteen years younger than me.

I also cried on the way back home from the shoot.

Some time ago, I overheard a conversation between two women in a coffee shop. One of them exclaimed, 'Oh my goodness! You have SO many friends!' The other seemed to visibly puff up with pride and replied, 'Yes I do.' It immediately made me want to take inventory of the number of people I would categorize as a friend.

> **Note to self:** You win some you lose some. I allow myself to feel bad about failure but I am not afraid of it. My failure in one arena doesn't blind me to the fact that I am successful in others.

I put down the book I was reading and stared into space. As I got ready to puff up with pride myself, it occurred to me that I only have a handful. Absolute treasures but nevertheless a handful. This got me thinking about all the people who had come and gone from my life. Of course, I was focusing more on the ones who had 'gone' from my life. I often say that I am a pattern recognition software and instinctively I started looking for a pattern in this.

I thought about all the relationships I have rejected and realized every single one had suffered the same fate on the grounds that there had been no honesty. It's a pity that honesty is such a rare trait. Do we tend to sacrifice honesty in the face of diplomacy? If so, where does one draw the line?

I don't regret the fact that I turned away from these people because I have always given people enough rope. In fact, my close friends say that I give people enough rope to hang themselves and their entire family tree – which is exactly what some people did before I realized my threshold of tolerance for dishonesty had finally been breached. And when that happens, I walk away with nary a regret.

Am I too finicky? Perhaps I would be better off turning a blind eye to the lies and false platitudes and the gossip or denial of gossip. But I'm not wired that way. I cannot respect someone who lies to cover up their mistakes. Wouldn't a mature person have the courage to stand up and say, 'Oops! That was a mistake. I'm sorry'? (And if admitting openly in so many words that one is fallible hurts the ego so much, even an 'Oops' would do the trick, wouldn't it?)

So no lies? Of course not. What sane person would be able to live in a completely true world? I don't claim to be a saint. And I am familiar with 'Oops'. The trick is to know the difference between white lies and damaging ones. And I do believe that to a large extent I've got the difference down pretty clearly in my head. At every stage in my life, I've done my best to be honest where it mattered. Aha! Where it mattered. I sat up straight. So that's where the mismatch occurs.

The chatter of the two women faded into the background as I made this particular discovery. This was my Eureka moment. I wondered how many people had felt that I hadn't met *their* standards of honesty. But then, does it matter?

> **Note to self:**
> Honesty is a matter of perception and opinion and the result of an assessment of consequences.

I glanced again at the women and one of them caught my eye. 'Waiting for someone?' her eyes asked me in that pitying way that people automatically seem to employ when they see a woman sitting alone in a coffee shop. I wanted to tell them my thoughts but I wasn't sure they would have understood my contentment. So I just smiled and went back to my book.

BEING A WOMAN

My approach to the world in general has to a large extent been influenced by the way my parents brought me up. As I mentioned earlier, my gender never played a role in determining whether I could or couldn't do something. The questions my parents always asked me were: Should you do it? Is it the right thing? But never 'Is it okay for you to do this as a girl?'

So I grew up blissfully unaware of gender discrimination. And because I didn't think it existed, it actually didn't for me. When someone told me I couldn't do something because I was a girl, I simply proved them wrong.

> **Note to self:**
> Perception is reality.
> And perception can
> be programmed.

Of course, I accept physical limitations.

I am a student of Kalaripayattu and have performed stunts in my shoots for my TV serial *Rekha IPS*. But I realize I am more easily injured than my male counterparts so I am always careful. But I don't say I cannot do something because I am a woman. I've done reverse flips, rope work and fight sequences and I think I've done it to the best of my abilities. Maybe a man could have done it better –

then again another woman could also have done it better.

At the risk of being beaten up by some women, I do believe we are the weaker sex. But only physically and that too when directly pitted against a man in something physical, like an arm-wrestling match, for instance. Not mentally, and definitely not emotionally. Show me a man who can run a household, deal with the domestic help, take care of kids and juggle a career and I'll keel over unconscious. You may say that there are such gloriously capable male specimens ... maybe, but I am yet to see one. We are more capable of dealing with demands on our time. We are more capable of handling demands. Period. Because I believe that we have so much to give. Maybe I am wrong but that wouldn't be a first.

I remember I was once asked to talk about gender inclusivity during a women's day programme and I couldn't do it. In order to talk about gender inclusivity you have to feel excluded in the first place; I've never felt so in my entire life.

There are many questions that are asked of a woman and my responses vary as I don different caps. Questions about freedom of choice, oppression and gender limitations are more pertinent when it comes to uneducated, marginalized women and my responses are different when I am talking for them or to them. But when I talk about my own experiences I say this: Isn't it time we stopped moaning about the fact that we are women and that the world is unfair to us? Why don't we simply focus on being the best we can be instead of whining about what can't be changed and doesn't need to be changed in the first place?

We all find ways of coping, I suppose. But sometimes I wonder if we sacrifice too much in order to do so. As I watch other women cope with their lives and see each one don a particular role in order to belong, I often feel as though I am on the fringes. I don't belong to the group of giggling girls nor do I belong to those elegantly coiffed women who whisper about one another with a malicious gleam in their eyes. And I don't identify with women who pretend to be airheads because it is the easiest way to get through life; all they talk about is clothes, jewellery and shopping. I wonder if they realize that life has a dangerous attribute: you become what you act and before you know it the image has become the reality.

This, I think, is where the struggle begins. The giggling girls want to grow up and be taken seriously, so they latch on to another image. Invariably it tilts either towards the sensuous or the philosophical. Somehow, in their minds, this is the path to be adopted if one wants to be taken seriously. So out come the cleavage-displaying dresses and body-hugging t-shirts, the pouting lips and swaying hips. And the other half spout the learnings of whoever the current philosophical icon is. The elegantly coiffed women, who have been continuously putting down others, discover that some of the women in their group have turned against them and then it becomes internecine. This group of women, I've noticed, is rather like amoeba – they split, form a whole with new members, and split again.

The third group is what interests me. In their infinite wisdom they've decided to *pretend* to be dumb so that their men feel less threatened. And then the genuinely dumb ones enter the group, who are nice but don't really play a role. The women hang out together when they are not at home. If they are well off, shopping is the prime focus, otherwise there are TV soaps and tabloid gossip. And one day, I believe, these women forget they were once intelligent and sometimes rational creatures. Of course I generalize; not all women are like this, but I have seen many who have lost their way.

I wish they would realize that it is intelligent to keep varying your roles. You can be anything you want to be. But only for a while. Then you change it. For this you have to be constantly conscious of the role you're playing as well as the reasons for doing so. Your basic intelligence dictates how effective you are and the success rate is never hundred per cent. But a little awareness goes a long way.

We have an immense ability to change. And this is because we have the ability to pick one emotion or feeling from a seething cauldron and focus on it, and let that dictate our response to the situation at hand in our lives. Erratic behaviour? Perhaps. But when it is accompanied by awareness, the behaviour is more deliberate and less frivolous. And when you are aware, you can be anything you want.

It is only when women forget they are playing a role that there is chaos. Each role is a road with a finite end. And before each end is a fork that takes you along a different route. It is awareness that saves you from reaching the end of a road.

> **Note to self:** We all have roles to play in life. But we must choose wisely, for if you act a part long enough, the part consumes you.

Be dumb. Enjoy the comfort. Be smart. Enjoy the confidence. Be a gossip and enjoy the malice. Be sweet and enjoy the cuddling. Be more of a man and confuse the heck out of everyone!

Or you can be an observer as well as a participant in your life. You can come and join me in the fringes...

But being on the fringes does mean you are never completely accepted anywhere. The way I look at it, not belonging completely is actually an advantage. I can transform from being a strong independent woman to a nervous helpless creature if that's what's going to get the work done. Yes, I know – I have a million women protesting indignantly at my statement, but think for a minute before you bash me up.

Consider the roads in India. Driving on the roads of Madras is quite an experience.

I used to drive a Scorpio, and I loved driving it. If the Scorpio were a man, I'd have found the perfect one. Darkly handsome, unintimidated ... you get the picture. Numerous trips down the East Coast Road in Madras have netted a range of experiences. Usually when I drive I have music playing. I drum on the wheel, shake my head and sing loudly. Since my windows are not tinted, I am under the constant gaze of those who drive past me. Either they are entertained or they are worriedly contemplating the consequences of allowing a lunatic behind the wheel. Needless to say, I am oblivious to either reaction. But there are occasions when youngsters who have had one too many have their male egos bruised when I overtake them. Some of them give chase and I usually ignore them and let them go. But if they honk too loud or if I am in a pugilistic mood, I plonk myself in the middle of the road and drive at a maddeningly sedate pace. When I think I have irritated them long enough I make an exaggerated move to the side and widely gesture at them to overtake my car. Cheap thrills, you know.

I deploy the same attitude when people honk at me to take a left turn when it is not a free left turn, or when they want me to move forward while the light is still red and there are four seconds to go. I stubbornly wait until the light turns green, regardless of whether there is traffic or not. I've had people cursing me as though I don't know how to drive, simply because I don't break the rules. But I have driven a car for the past twenty years without incident and I am not going to give in to the pressure to conform to bad behaviour.

There's one tactic that works like magic for me when people are not giving way. I usually drive in a very relaxed way, leaning back comfortably in the seat. But if I need someone to give way, I lean forward and clutch the steering wheel with a very nervous look on my face. The other drivers take one look at my body language and give me a wide berth. It's hilarious to see the alacrity with which they give way. The stereotype about women drivers works admirably at these times. I maintain this body language until I have overtaken them and then go back to my usual relaxed way of driving.

See what I meant about changing into a woman I am not in order to get my way?

> **Note to self:**
> Pretending to fit a stereotype sometimes gets the job done. Must remember not to overuse it lest it loses its effectiveness.

Psssst! I do it on other occasions too but I have found that smiling sweetly does the trick just as well.

But there are some occasions where smiling sweetly doesn't work. And that is when you are handling eve-teasing. I must confess that the number of incidents has gone down in the past few years but men will always be boys. Also, let's admit it, I am older now.

Until a few years ago, I faced some amount of unwanted attention. It was another hot summer morning and I was determinedly pounding along the track, burning calories. I have always loved this part of my day. When I jog I meet people from various walks of life and despite the fact that we don't really know each other, greetings are exchanged. It is as though just by coming to the YMCA to work out, we automatically belong to a family and there are no strangers. At least that is how it has always been in all the years I have been going there.

That morning was different. The previous day had been one of my 'I don't care, I will eat what I want and as much as I want' days. Naturally, guilt had crept in by morning and I set myself a target of eight kilometres. I began jogging at a controlled pace and the first lap went like any other – I said hello to the other morning walkers, someone asked me how many laps I was going to do, another commented that I was losing weight, yet another said she liked my show, two guys stared at me in surprise as they cycled past, whispering, 'Dei, Anu Hasan da... Anu Hasan...' Like I said, it was like any other day.

As I began the second lap, I noticed a car parked near the wall of the golf course adjoining the YMCA. As I jogged past, I saw smoke curling out of the open windows and I wondered how anyone could be smoking first thing in the morning. The guys in the car were probably wondering how anyone could be jogging in this heat. Well, if I were one of them, that's what I would have thought. I continued jogging.

When I came around on my third lap, the guys in the car had recognized me and decided to pass comments. The first one was about my uncle, which I ignored. The next one was about my show, which also I paid no attention to. By then I had passed them and didn't hear any more. But when I came back around for the fourth lap, they commented on my running style and the shape of my body and THAT was something I was not going to ignore.

Without hesitating, I turned around and jogged back to the car, stuck my face into the window and said, 'This is not the place to park your car, smoke and pass comments. It really isn't nice.' And without waiting for their reply, I jogged away.

From their startled expressions, it was clear that they had not expected me to confront them. Like a proper demure Indian woman, I was meant to look away and turn a blind eye to their bad behaviour.

I seethe at the thought that educated people waste their time in this way. It was six-thirty in the morning for heaven's sake! If they were from the street, I would have excused them for they don't know better. Not that I wouldn't have confronted them if I thought their actions warranted it. But it saddens me to see educated young men do this kind of thing. Of what use their education? Of what use the fancy car?

After I had finished my laps, I spotted a police constable

on a bike. I was tempted to tell him there were some guys sitting in a car and that he should book them for eve-teasing. But this Eve had better things to do. Besides, I didn't want to get involved in the hassle of a police case just so I could exact pointless revenge on some fellows who didn't know better. After all, if they couldn't be bothered to toss that cigarette (not to mention their attitude) and join the rest of us in our quest for good health, it was their loss, not mine. In any case I did walk up to the car and confront them. And I hope that I made them pause to think.

There have been many incidents on the road and in the trains in India where I confronted men who tried to misbehave (for want of a better – or worse – word). Once in Calcutta, in the metro, there was this huge chap in a pathan suit. Throughout the journey I felt his beady eyes on me and noticed that he was edging closer to me. When I reached my stop fifteen minutes later, I was on high alert. I just knew this guy was going to try something.

As I stepped out of the tube, he made his move. He reached across and tried to pinch my bottom. I was moving too fast and all he managed to do was tug my kurta. Without breaking my stride, I pivoted on the foot I had set on the platform, stepped back into the crowded train, grabbed his shirt front and said, 'Lay a finger on me and you will be in really deep trouble.'

It was a crowded train and I knew he wouldn't dare do anything. Plus this was Calcutta. Before he could react I stepped off the train and watched the doors swing shut. Then I turned and walked away. When I narrated this incident to some female friends of mine in Calcutta they said it was

Note to self: Don't let the small misdemeanours slide. If you do, they become acceptable and the level continues to escalate.

too confrontational and not very 'ladylike'. But I knew I couldn't let it go. Maybe I nipped things in the bud, maybe I didn't. But at least I didn't do nothing.

At the same time I urge women to always stay safe. I have been asked if I learnt Kalaripayattu so I could beat up men who misbehave. Which, I think, is a stupid question. I will confront when I can. But if I am threatened, my first reaction will always, always be to extricate myself. And if I have no way out, I won't go down quietly. I will take as many as I can with me. But for that you don't need to know Kalari, sheer rage will suffice.

CATS AND DOGS

I am an unabashed animal lover. My mum says she is always worried that I will go to Masai Mara one day, see a lion and go 'How sweet!', walk up for a cuddle and get mauled. Thankfully for her, I have never had the opportunity to do so.

I have always been a people-watcher. Different personalities, behaviours, attitudes... I find all this quite fascinating. Oddly enough, I notice the same thing in animals. All the pets we've had displayed remarkable human traits. As a result I'd like to think that they taught me lessons too.

Whenever I see a black and white cat, I think of Swamiji. No, this is not some guru or godman. It was the name of our cat. He would spend hours staring soulfully at the picture of Lord Venkateshwara in my parents' puja room. I had seen many cats but such a spiritual one I had never laid eyes on. Hence the name. We later discovered that he was no swamiji but a patient hunter. There was a window behind the picture through which squirrels entered the puja room to scrounge for things to eat. All he was doing was waiting

> **Note to self:** First impressions, however logically deduced, need not be right.

patiently for the next unsuspecting squirrel to come in, so he could pounce on it. A hunter he might have been but Swamiji he remained.

At one point we had nine cats in our house. Mapposcat was the grande dame and our first cat. Then came Swamiji and Dorian Grey. Dorian Grey had three kittens that were creatively named Blackie I, Blackie II and Spitfire. Then there were three other strays who were occasional visitors. Each of these cats had a distinct personality with clear likes and dislikes. One liked crisp biscuits, another liked them soggy, one liked warm milk and another liked cream in it.

Dorian Grey was the snootiest cat I've ever known. When she was hungry, she would sit at the entrance to the kitchen and stare silently at my mother. It was beneath her dignity to mew in order to get my mother's attention. Dorian Grey only had soggy biscuits with her milk. I remember once my mother placed some biscuits on a small plate. Dorian walked up to it, sniffed at it disdainfully, looked up at my mother with accusing eyes and stalked away. I still remember my mother calling out to her in apology.

Swamiji was a cat with a number of peculiarities that my mother found almost obscene. I always found him cute. I think he was gay. He used to play mother to Blackie I, II and Spitfire, groom them, play with them, etc., while Dorian Grey traipsed around the neighbourhood flirting with the other tomcats.

One morning we noticed Swamiji walking around with a sharp pointy tail. On looking closer we realized he had licked it and shaped it into a point. My mother was disgusted. I found it hilarious. He maintained this style for the next few days and I warned my mother that he would soon start curling his tail or maybe even tie it in a bow. Some days later, when we came back home after dinner, we noticed that every one of our cats had a pointy tail. I collapsed into laughter while my mother gave Swamiji a good scolding and told him to never do that again to the other cats (although it took my mother's constant vigil for the next two weeks before he gave up attempting the pointy tail style on the others!).

Spitfire was the one who was attached to my father. Whenever my dad started packing, she would jump onto the bed, dive into his suitcase and curl up inside. My father would patiently lift her out and continue packing. She was quite the drama queen. Just when my dad had shut the suitcase and lifted it off the bed, she would fall at his feet and mew plaintively. Of course my father would melt. He'd bend down, pick her up and cuddle her and tell her he was sorry and leave the house reluctantly for his trip. And the moment he stepped out of the door, our little drama queen would go curl up on the pillow on the bed and go off to sleep. So much for her plaintive mews.

Jokes apart, I think in some ways, Spitfire taught me how to live in the moment.

The three kittens – they were a riot. They liked having breakfast at 10 a.m. While on weekdays this wasn't a problem, on Sundays it was. My mother liked to watch *Ramayan* on the television. So when the three came to ask her for food, she'd tell

Note to self: Be happy when you have reason to be. Your regret at losing something should not let you forget that life goes on.

them 'I've put the milk there ... near the kitchen. Drink that and when I finish watching this I will come and give you some biscuits.' Yes, we all conversed with our cats and I like to believe they understood us.

I think they did inspect the milk once and decided it was not to their specifications. The next thing we knew, they had discovered that jumping on the TV stabilizer dislodged the power plug for the TV. The first time they did that, my mother worried for their safety. But to her indignation, they started doing it the next Sunday as well. The third Sunday saw my mother watching *Ramayan* with a big walking stick. The moment the kittens stepped into the living room, she frenziedly banged the stick on the floor, yelling, 'No no no,' until they skittered away. I wish I had videoed that. My mother – not the kittens.

When I look back I don't recall how we stopped having cats. I only remember leaving a house with many cats and returning to one with none. Did they die? Run away? Get thrown out in a sack? I wonder if I should ask my mother.

No. My memories are only those that make me smile. Why stain them with those of death and loss?

If I am a coward, at least I am a happy coward. About the cats. But not the dog. And he was the best dog in the whole world.

As years went by, I didn't have the opportunity to keep pets. Until my first marriage.

My then husband had a dog named Shogun. He was a German Shepherd and a very handsome beast. Incredibly large and incredibly clever. I completely adored Shogun. So much so the business was named after him.

Shogun was a delight. When we used to go for walks, he would ignore me but when I went and hid behind a tree, he would realize I wasn't there and start a panicked search for me. When I emerged from behind a tree grinning, he would coolly look away, his demeanour would change at once from panic-stricken to casual as if to say, I wasn't worried you weren't there. I don't care. But I knew he did. This was a game we played.

Then there was the 'Who did it'. This was a phrase which made Shogun look guilty regardless of whether he had done something or not. I would walk into a room and ask who did it and Shogun would look guilty and try and make himself invisible. It was hilarious the first few times but I stopped doing it after a while when I realized it wasn't funny any more. I did cling to the memories of those first few times and chuckle.

But what amazed me was how Shogun reacted to Abe. He had always been protective of me around men and so when Abe visited, I warned Abe that he should give Shogun time to get used to him. I told him Shogun would growl at him but if he let him sniff his fingers, he would be fine. Abe agreed.

He walked into the room and I stood between him and Shogun, my hand on Shogun's collar. He looked at Shogun and said in an incredibly gentle loving voice, 'Hello, sweetheart' and Shogun just melted! His ears went flat and he walked up to Abe and licked his hand! I couldn't believe my eyes.

And when Priya (a fellow BITsian

Note to self: Never underestimate the power of love – it does soothe the savage beast.

and a good friend) and her husband Ram moved to Calcutta, Shogun had a new home to go to when we travelled. He had always hated being left behind, in a kennel, so having this option made him a happy dog. He loved playing with Priya and Ram and would quickly climb into their car when they came to pick him up.

He loved pretty women and would fawn all over Sarika (my aunt) when she visited us. But when I brought in a dirty-looking woman or a man wearing a turban, he would go berserk and bark his head off.

As you can see, he gave me many a delightful moment.

But with age, Shogun's health deteriorated. The vet told us that we were being cruel by prolonging his life. He had lost bladder and bowel control. And I could see the wounded pride in Shogun's eyes when he sat in his own feces, unable to get up.

I would gently move him and clean him during those times but when we realized that he had also got skin cancer, the vet advised us to put him to sleep.

I sat with him while the doctor gave him the final injection. He died peacefully, his head on my lap.

I knew he had to go and I knew we were doing what we thought was best at the time.

It is odd that the marriage died shortly after Shogun did. Now, so many years later, I wonder if it was perhaps Shogun who taught me to let go.

Note to self:
Lessons come from unlikely sources. And the realization might come after several years, after you have actually learnt and implemented the lessons.

LESSONS FROM WORK

The camera and I have always had an on-off relationship. I started my sojourn with films and TV with the lead role in *Indira*, a Tamil movie, in 1993–94. While the movie went on to win the Best International Film Award at the Belarus Film Festival, I did not use that to clamber up the ladder. In fact I didn't act for about seven years after *Indira*. Actresses in India typically stop acting when they get married and then go back to acting when they get divorced. My career path may look like it fits this stereotype but when you look closely, there are differences.

I never wanted a career in front of the camera, even before I realized where my core competencies lay. One question I am often asked is this: 'Why didn't you act after *Indira*?' Well, I did get offers after *Indira* but nothing came of them. I had my reasons, along with some conditions. No skimpy clothes. No heavy romance. No dancing around trees. For a heroine who was one-film-old, these were a helluva lot of conditions. So the producers went away, saying they would think about it. I think they are still thinking about it!

I went on to get married, started a business, returned to acting in television, worked as a line producer for a film, got divorced, started another business, started to work in front of the camera again before selling off the business, got married again and moved to London. The return to acting came before the divorce and was uninfluenced by the fact that my marriage was on shaky grounds.

And no matter what work I did, at every stage I was taught lessons.

The first set of learning came from the business I started. At that time I was still married and since my (now ex) husband was posted in Calcutta, we decided to start a business there. It was a marketing company and what started off as a four member team grew into a 130-employee company. I must, in all fairness, admit that while I laid the foundation, the credit for growing it to the size it eventually became was my ex-husband's and not mine.

The core team consisted of Tarun, Asitendu, Pallab and Sangeeta and, later, Mrityunjoy. I smile when I think of them. All of them joined me as sales executives for a paltry salary of 2,500 rupees a month plus commission.

Tarun was the melodramatic but emotional one, Asitendu was slow and steady, Pallab was cheeky and Sangeeta was fiercely loyal and hardworking. Mrityunjoy was a combination of all these traits and one of the sincerest people I have ever seen. When I was recruiting them I did not look for how much they knew; I looked for their willingness to learn.

They came in as freshers and learnt on the job. And so did I, along with them. I am still in touch with

Note to self:
Attitude is always more important than aptitude. Or, as they say, EQ is as significant if not more than IQ.

them. When I hear about how well they are doing, I feel a rush of pride. So my approach had been right after all.

While I was busy learning how to market, push sales and monitor quality control, I also learnt to deal with fraud. We were marketing credit cards for Citibank and there were strict document guidelines that we had to follow when sourcing applications. When the pressure for sales increased, the ones who could not meet their target started looking at other means of achieving them. One of the most popular methods was to beg for applications to be accepted with incorrect documentation. This I could handle easily enough. But there was a far more serious issue that I had to contend with and that was falsification of documents.

I had trained Sangeeta on quality control and she was as eagle-eyed as I was when it came to identifying fraud. She came to me one day with an income tax document. I knew right away what she had found. The document had been altered in order to meet the income requirements. It had been done by one of our employees who had not been coming in to work very regularly.

I called him into my room, pushed the income tax document across the table and asked, 'Do you have anything to say about this?'

He tried to act cool and said, 'What is it, ma'am?'

I held on to my temper and decided to test him. I said, 'I have spoken to the customer and he is faxing me a copy of his IT document.' I waited. He said nothing. 'You do realize this can become a police case.' Again, no response.

'Why did you do it?' I said at last. 'I am so disappointed.' The moment I said that a dam broke. He broke down and

> **Note to self:** There are times when an honest confrontation has more power to reach an individual than a Machiavellian one.

confessed and promised never to do it again. And true to his word, he never did. He resigned the next month.

I felt sorry for him when he resigned but he had the grace to come and talk to me about it. He was going to join his father in the foundry business and he didn't think he could cut it as a sales executive. I wished him luck and sent him on his way.

I suppose when you run a business these kinds of situations are par for the course. A few years later, my ex-husband came across one of those data-processing opportunities. (Eventually we discovered it was a scam.) The core members of that team were Priyojit and, later, Suborna. Priyojit always struck me as philosophical yet emotional, an observant and responsible boy. During his watch, so to speak, two of the executives decided to cheat. I was tempted to fire them but I called Priyojit and asked him what he thought I should do.

He wanted me to give them another chance. And I did. In doing so, I emphasized my trust not in the fact that they would change but in the fact that I respected Priyojit's judgement. And it was spot on. He was, until the very end, one of the most trustworthy and diligent leaders I have ever known.

Rewinding a few years back into the marketing company, I spent all of the first year running after targets, maintaining quality control, giving motivational speeches and figuring out incentive schemes. I had to make this business work because this was to be our bread and butter after my ex-husband quit the army. I worked long hours and obsessed over every detail. I handled recruitments to manage the loss in manpower. I designed advertisements, interviewed people, trained them while I monitored existing teams. I worked really hard.

> **Note to self:** It is important to know when trust imbibes a greater sense of responsibility and when it gives irresponsibility a free rein.

Even I am impressed with myself that I did so much. But I paid the price. In the midst of all this I had forgotten to get my accounts in shape. Suddenly it was time to file tax returns and my paperwork was in shambles. I spent hours poring over bank statements and trying to balance the books. Somehow, with the help of a chartered accountant, I managed to get everything in place but it wasn't easy. That is when I reluctantly learnt my second most important lesson: delegate delegate delegate.

I employed an accountant. I gave Tarun, Asitendu and Mrityunjoy more responsibility and they shone through. Sangeeta took charge of the QC department as well as training and she was flawless. This left me free to deal with incentive schemes, retaining employees, meeting sales targets, liaising with the bank and overseeing the accountant.

The second year was much better. We started making money while maintaining high standards of quality. I used to din into all my employees something that was a core belief in me – there are no shortcuts in life. I

> **Note to self:** It is not always true that if you want a job done well, you have to do it yourself.

didn't realize how much of an impact it had on them. Today when I speak to them, they tell me what they remember the most is the importance I placed on honesty. At a time where everyone is trying to make themselves appear better than they really are, I insisted that it is best to show yourself for what you are. Even if it is in a job interview. Your trust in your ability, as well as your faith that you can learn what you do not know, is more convincing than a false representation of your skill set.

The years went by. My ex-husband quit the army and joined the business. He took over marketing and business development and I took over HR and administration. I had formed quite an attachment to the core group of employees and watched over them carefully, ensuring their growth was commensurate with the results they brought in.

One of the first people to leave was Sangeeta. The business was being controlled by my ex-husband, whose core values and approach to work were very different from mine. I am not saying he was 'wrong' but when you are used to a particular style of management, sometimes a different style makes it difficult to hang on.

I started acting in TV and films again and slowly withdrew more and more from the day-to-day operations of the business. I began to realize I was comfortable when I was facing the camera. I never thought I was particularly gifted or beautiful. But I do believe I brought sincerity to my work before the camera. Most of my roles in television those days were that of the strong but wronged woman. It was fun for a while. I never really wanted to be a star and, honestly, I never was.

We were filming in Mahabalipuram. For those of you who don't know, this is a crowded beach resort near Madras. The heat was unbearable. We were waiting for the shot to be set up. As is the custom, all the artists sat together and chatted idly while a bus load of tourists embarked and made a bee line for the camera.

The attitude of people towards filming in those days was quite amusing. Some gawked openly. Others – especially young boys – pretended nonchalance and spoke in loud voices or made rude remarks. Others still swarmed up to the actors and asked for photographs and autographs.

One of them got an autograph from my co-star and then came to me. I was both flattered and embarrassed but I wasn't about to let either emotion show. So, with a coolness I didn't possess, I signed my name. As I handed back his little book, he asked me, 'What is your name?'

As my work took me to Madras more and more, back in Calcutta, my core team weakened in their conviction to stay on at the company. When Sangeeta wanted to leave for a better opportunity, we had a very honest conversation. I ensured that she was indeed going for something that would be better and I bid her goodbye, wishing her well. I know she would have been an asset if she stayed on but it was not good for her personal growth if she did. Besides, she needed to be where she was appreciated.

> **Note to self:** Being in the limelight might go to your head but there will always be moments that remind you to keep your feet firmly on the ground. Pay heed to them.

When the data-processing arm of the company started,

Note to self: While employee retention is important, you have to put your conscience before your business and do what is right for your employee.

I threw myself into setting it up as devotedly as I had when it came to setting up the marketing business. But what I had hammered into my employees I couldn't drill into my then husband – that there were no shortcuts in life. I stood back and watched him go at it while deep inside I knew it wasn't going to work out. The whole thing turned out to be a scam and the 'license fee' that we paid disappeared along with the 'business partner' we had signed up with. By then I had acceded to my ex-husband's desire to get into film production and was on my way to being line producer for *Mumbai Xpress*. I left Calcutta for that. Little did I realize that I would never return.

My memories of that phase are shrouded with guilt, apathy, helplessness and other negative emotions. When I spoke to Priyojit recently, he said when I left I had known that we were not going to land the data-processing project. In those words I sensed a gentle reprimand. But I had been struggling through a very difficult time in my life and had to focus on keeping my head above the water. Yes, I was a rat and I was deserting a sinking ship. But the ship I was deserting was that of my marriage and not the business. Leaving the business and the employees I had come to care about was collateral damage. I don't know exactly what happened to the company after that but I think every one of those employees drifted on to other jobs with no great drama or trauma. And some of them are doing very well indeed. If I had blown open the fact that we were never going to make things work, it would have caused unnecessary panic and perhaps even damaged the business prospects that my ex-husband later managed to bring to fruition in the marketing and real estate side of the business.

As for me, while I moved from active involvement in the company to being the line producer of *Mumbai Xpress*, the bilingual movie produced by Raajkamal Films International, I was thrown into a situation I had never been in before. I had all the responsibility I could handle but less of the authority I was used to and none of the autonomy I had until now taken for granted.

I made mistakes. Lots of them.

My uncle Kamal (Kamal Haasan) had said he wanted a crane on top of a building for a particular scene in the movie. I spoke to the production manager and he said it wasn't a problem. I double-checked with a family friend of mine, who was in the construction business, and he too said there was no problem. But when we landed in Mumbai, there *was* one. You see, Kamal wanted a tower crane and all this while we had thought he wanted a regular one. I got a sick feeling in my stomach as I understood our mistake.

I remember facing Kamal in his room. The production managers were standing next to me, staring at their feet. I was shouted at. I was mortified. From being the boss of my own company I had to get used to being an employee, and an inept one at that, if my uncle's wrath was anything to go by. I have been many things, including an employee, but inept is not one of them.

I waited until I could leave the room and yelled at the managers. I am sure they yelled at someone else in turn. But all the yelling in the world didn't change the fact that we hadn't delivered what the boss wanted. Of course, the boss could have been clearer in his instructions but only a poor tradesman blames his tools, remember? I wasn't going to look for excuses. I scrambled around and finally managed to get in touch with someone at a construction company and found a tower crane on top of a thirty-storey, under-construction building.

We paid a fortune to be allowed to film there but I did get Kamal what he wanted.

Note to self: If something goes wrong, there is no point wallowing in self-pity or trying to apportion blame. Get cracking and find a solution.

But I became much more cautious about taking instructions from Kamal after that. He has this tendency to skip sentences, probably because his brain works much faster than he can communicate. He thinks we are capable of hearing sentences one and four and able to fill in the logical content of the sentences inbetween.

So I made lists. I asked questions even if it made him impatient. I checked and double-checked what he wanted. This approach worked and I didn't make any major mistakes after that.

By the time I finished working on *Mumbai Xpress*, I was clear about one thing: being the person I was, I was not happy being a line producer. And that was also when another thing became clear – my marriage simply wasn't working. But I shall speak about that in a different section. For now, I'll stick to lessons from work.

I acted in TV serials, films, anchored shows and even set

up a juice and smoothies business, ran it and later sold it. With each new thing I did, I discovered a side to myself that surprised me, pleased me and sometimes disappointed me.

> **Note to self:** Once the solution to a mistake has been found and applied, THAT is the time to analyse why it happened in the first place and ensure it doesn't happen again.

I have always prided myself on being professional. Of course there are many who would probably say that I carry professionalism a bit too far. But I have no regrets about doing that.

I am normally nice to people who are competent (and nasty to those who are not ... and that's a personal failing I am working on). There have been times when I wished that people who were not as competent would learn from their mistakes and apply it to their working style. But you know what they say, learning a lesson and applying it are two different things.

I was acting in a film and we were shooting the climax sequence. Being the climax, naturally the scene was one where we were standing out in the blistering heat, watching the hero beat up the baddies. To add to the effect, there were giant propeller fans throwing up dust and mud at our faces.

We were all miserable. Every breath I took seemed laden with mud and I cringed at the thought of what my lungs were having to go through. My feet were filthy and I avoided looking at them after the first few hours. There was mud everywhere – in our eyes, nose, ears! And to make matters worse, I was supposed to cry during the entire sequence. While it is possible to whip oneself into a frenzy of tears when you have a few well-written dialogues, it is well nigh impossible for me to maintain the emotion for four days when all I am doing is inhaling dirt. So I had to resort to glycerine, a first for me, because I usually prefer to get into the mood and feel real emotion.

I am a complete wimp when it comes to putting glycerine in my eyes. I take a deep breath and stick my finger into my eye and then do a war dance while the darn thing stings like crazy. So there I was, in the climax sequence, with a sticky face, braving the mud and dirt, when my co-artist told me, 'I am taking my clothes home with me and washing them. You know these costumiers, they will claim to have washed it when they haven't.'

The thought of wearing the same dirty clothes the next day was too much to contemplate, so I immediately decided I would do the same and with a noble air told the costumier, 'I will save you the extra work of washing my sari. I will wash it and bring it tomorrow to shoot.' The costumier looked suitably relieved and off I went in my grubby clothes.

I reached home and threw the clothes into the washing machine and fiddled around with the dial. The usual cycle was one-and-a-half hours. I decided the clothes needed a good scrubbing and set it on a three-hour cycle. Then I traipsed off to revert to human mode from dirty piglet mode. It is unbelievable how good it feels to get clean after having spent the whole day the way I had.

Three hours later, I came humming back to the machine and pulled out the clothes and had the shock of my life. The fall of the sari had run colour and, what had been a cream-coloured border, was now dull brown. I was aghast.

I had the climax shoot the next day and for someone who prided herself in being professional, this was the most unprofessional thing I could have done!

I called up the associate director and his first response was, 'Oh dear, why did you take it home!' I felt terribly guilty even as I began to mentally list the various ways to tackle the problem: attach a new border, buy an identical sari, etc. But I knew I had to call the director and apologize. I was thoroughly ashamed of myself.

The director came on the line and as I started to tell him what I had done, I had to hold back my tears. His reaction was surprisingly cool. He immediately said he would send the costumier to my house and we would see what needed to be done for the next day's shoot.

The costumier came home and I apologized profusely and said I didn't know the fall would run colour. A part of me was tempted to blame him for not washing the fall before attaching it to the sari but if I could be noble and claim I was saving extra work for him when all I was saying was that I didn't trust him to do his job, I could be noble when I messed up.

The next day, when I reached the shoot location, I was still writhing with guilt and I went over to the director's caravan and apologized again. I was wearing the now slightly different sari and a chastized expression.

The director smiled at me and said, 'The sari is not too bad. Just that the border is a few shades darker than when we started. So it's okay, we can manage.' I apologized again and he responded, 'We are shooting the climax. If during such a dramatic climax, the audience ends up noticing that the colour of your sari border is darker by a few shades then we have really failed as film-makers, haven't we?'

The professional in me recognized the statement for what it was – a sop to my wounded ego. But the wounded ego and the guilt grabbed the proffered excuse and calmed down. I felt a rush of gratitude for the way the director had handled the crisis. I walked out of the caravan with a lighter heart. Another apology to the costumier and my raging guilt somewhat quietened.

> **Note to self:**
> Professionalism is not about being right and correct all the time. It is also about being able to handle other people's mistakes in the right way.

I will never be completely rid of the guilt. Nor will I forget the lesson the director taught me.

A lesson learnt – yet to be applied.

People say you have to experience life in order to learn. But in one particular area I knew the lesson even without it being taught to me. I have always steered clear of getting involved with colleagues at work. I have seen romance blossoming between co-artists. Some have resulted in marriage, some in heartbreak while others have been relegated to no more than a momentary aberration. I have never understood what makes people gamble away their happiness on something that begins as an illusion. Is it courage or foolhardiness that makes them do so?

There were occasions when I was reminded with unforgiving clarity that certain things were missing in my life and I had to accept the fact that it was out of my personal choice. You see, my life was – and still is – rich with happiness, glorious freedom and great friends that I would never trade for anything. So if there was a romantic hero missing in my life's script, it was because this character had not been scripted in. Or maybe I should say he had been scripted out.

When I was younger I harboured the usual fantasies about playing the role of a wife and mother to perfection. But as I grew older, my romantic fantasies faded. It was not for want of trying. My role was played well – but the screenplay and the casting went awry. I have been convinced for several years now that my psyche is unable to pay the price for that role, which so many women play so convincingly. So while I absolutely love men and even harboured romantic fantasies about some of them, somewhere I knew that permanence was not a part of my life.

But I believed that all that changed when I agreed to marry Graham. Marriage to him meant I still had my freedom and friends and I realized I didn't have to fit into any stereotype. Suddenly marriage seemed a desirable option once again.

While other single women may be reminded of the difference when they see other families, when I was single I had a tougher job. In my field of work, I've had to play the role of those very women I thought I could never be – a happy wife, a loving mother.

But when I play the role of a loving wife, my mind reminds me that the man against whom I lean comfortably

> **Note to self:**
> Sometimes our convictions are not the absolute truth, and it is good for the all-knowing mind to eat humble pie. I am certain life is going to offer me many more such opportunities in the future.

is a figment of someone else's imagination yet a part of my temporary reality, which will fade into the many other characters I have imagined.

I remember a particularly poignant role I once played. It was the part of a loving, happy wife. But she is in his life for a very short period and then she dies. The man playing the role of my husband was a good-looking man, charming and well-behaved. This external appearance that every woman finds attractive is the one I have to use as a tool to assist me in portraying my role. And I have to remind my brain that this is a role, that he is only a temporary reality as I hold his hand and he acts the part of a loving husband. I have to remember that, in my permanent reality, expectations and demands invariably drown out my sense of freedom. Expectations create pressure and I tend to give up elements of my freedom in order to meet them.

So while I play the role with conviction, my body language and the laughter in my eyes belie the control I exert over the boundaries within. A part of me watches dispassionately as the other settles convincingly into the role. The joy, laughter and affection all so real and yet time bound.

When the director yelled, 'Cut!' I could hear the satisfaction in his voice. My make-believe husband set aside the Power Ranger toy he had been using as a prop to narrate a story to my make-believe son. I had done a convincing job and so had he. As I stepped back from the scene I was enacting, I simultaneously withdrew from any lingering warmth. My job was done and I extended my hand for a firm handshake.

He said, 'A pleasure meeting you.'

'A pleasure working with you,' I replied, the professional firmly in control over the woman in me.

It was time for me to go home. Alone.

Living alone gave me a wonderful sense of freedom. But even I have to admit that it is a nuisance when people do not know the concept of being on time. (And before you say, 'And your point is?' I shall pre-empt the question and tell you, 'I'm getting there. I'm getting there.')

My pickup for shoot is usually early in the morning. I wake up much earlier and run off for my workout. I return from my workout with precisely twenty minutes to spare. I don't need more than fifteen minutes to shower, change and get ready to leave. But I digress.

> **Note to self:**
> When using your imagination to deliver a performance, never let the boundaries between imagination and reality blur.

I had a driver called Mohan who was punctual to the minute. I had given him instructions that he was to come and ring the bell on the dot, not earlier or later. Early would mean I was in the shower and since there was no one else to open the door, I would have the delightful experience of having to grit my teeth against the panic-stricken peals of the calling bell when no one opened the door on the very first summons. What is it with people and calling bells anyway? They ring once and if there is no immediate response they ring again and again in desperate fervour.

The first time Mohan fell ill, a new driver was sent to pick me up. This guy was given a pickup time of 7:45 a.m. He rang the bell at 7:30 to tell me he was there. I was about to step into the shower when I heard the bell. I quickly ran to the door and told him to wait and ring the bell again at 7:45. He said okay and went back downstairs. There he started chatting with the watchman and didn't come up. I called out from my balcony, 'Watchman! Is my driver there?' The guy came huffing up the stairs a good ten minutes later to help me carry my costume bag and other essential things I take with me when going for a shoot. One person could not carry everything to the car else I would have done it myself. We were late by ten minutes but this translated into a twenty-minute delay due to an increase in traffic. So I ended up doing my make-up in the car so that I could still be ready for my shoot at 9 a.m.

The next day the guy came to pick me up and did the same thing. I told him (with gritted teeth) that he should look at his watch and come and ring the bell at 7.45 a.m. Not before and not after. He said, 'Okay madam, sorry madam,' and once again we set off for the shoot with me finishing make-up in the car.

The next morning, when I came back to my apartment after my workout, I found the driver waiting outside the door. I went up to him and asked him to show me his watch. He did. I told him, 'See? It's 7.25 a.m. now. Look at your watch... When THIS needle comes HERE, you come up and ring the bell.' The driver said, 'Seri madam, seri madam,' and I ran up to shower and get ready. And what happens? He doesn't come up until ten minutes to eight. When I asked him why he was late, he said, 'Just five minutes, madam.' I got mad at that and told him I couldn't for the life of me understand why he couldn't come up on time. I wasted another five minutes, explaining to him why it was inconvenient if he arrived early and why he shouldn't be late. And yes. I did my make-up in the car that day.

It took me a while to realize that being punctual is considered an eccentricity. I now have an electric doorbell that I switch off when I cannot come to the door. And I call my production manager at pickup time to ask him where the car is. My stress levels are much lower. But I heard from another production house that no driver wants to come to pick me up. They believe I am too difficult because I insist they come on time, neither early nor late. I wasn't too bothered by this until my director asked me one day with a mocking smile, 'I believe you yell at them if they come even five minutes late?' I felt hurt at that, and then consoled myself and told him, 'What to do, I should have been in the military...'

I continue to remain punctual.

Of the many mistakes I made during my tenure as actress and TV presenter, one was showing how little I tolerated incompetence. It became a huge issue during a cookery show I was hosting/anchoring and we finally decided not to continue with it.

In retrospect, I suppose I should have allowed for the fact that the director was a mother and also managing other shows. But unfortunately, when it comes to work, I am unable to accept anything less than hundred per cent. So every

Note to self: Being punctual and disciplined shows character. It means you value other people's time like your own. It also means you get your work done and are super-productive.

time a shoot was delayed, or things went missing, someone handed me the wrong ingredients or missed a shot, my temper sizzled. The last straw was when the director pointed out that I had not read out the cookery tip. Actually I had – when she was talking on the phone while the camera was rolling. I said as much to her. It was not well received. Then, while I was waiting for the next shot to be set up, I saw her entire team laughing and joking instead of working. That's when I made my final mistake. I said loudly, 'If you are going to be joking and chatting, the work is not going to get done.' I should have worded it differently. I should have toned down the anger. I should have done many things. But I didn't.

This incident was the tipping point. When we brought it to the channel head's notice, he made it out to be just a case of two women being unable to work together. I was so angry I am ashamed to say that I actually cried. That only made the poor man uncomfortable. But what took me by surprise was what the director said next: 'I come from a good family. You spoke to me like I was someone beneath you. I have worked with that team for eight years and you insulted me.'

I couldn't understand how she could be so disorganized during a shoot but I did understand that my anger was insulting. I hadn't meant it to be. I was merely venting my frustration. I never regretted that I wound up that cookery show. But I regretted that I had failed to be diplomatic and had been rude. I apologized to her and felt a little better.

The fallout of the incident was that there was a lot of talk about me being difficult to work with. But I had worked with the other team on *Koffee* for nearly four years and apparently my director Mohan responded to the remarks by saying: 'If you know how to handle her, she is not difficult at all.' I smiled because it made me sound like a high-strung filly.

After that incident I tried not to lose my temper when I thought someone was careless or disinterested. To a large extent I succeeded. I also made sure I didn't work with people who struck me as incompetent. Thankfully there were more than enough people who were more competent than me, so I was never short of work. I continued to work in films and television and at one point I was so busy I was hopping cities the entire week. Believe me, it is not half as exciting as it sounds.

> **Note to self:** When you are more competent than another at work, aggressively highlighting the difference will not earn you praise for your abilities – it only earns you enemies.

One of my trips to Hyderabad for a film shoot got me thinking. How can a summer's day become wintry and cold and then brighten to spring all over again? In order to explain this whimsical question, I have to tell you the story.

The production team had been having glitches in their coordination from the start of the project so I was rather cautious about going all the way to Hyderabad as a guest of their rather questionable efficiency. Nevertheless work is work and commitments once made – at least in my book – have to be adhered to.

So I landed in Hyderabad and was somewhat mollified by the fact that the driver was there on time to pick me up and that the hotel room had been booked. Buoyed by this,

I went to bed and woke up my usual energetic self, ready for a full day's shoot.

Everything went well until lunch. I was famished. I trotted across to my caravan – they'd even ensured that I had a caravan all to myself! So you can't blame me for feeling just that bit complacent.

I entered the caravan and declared that I was famished and my assistant told me, 'Your lunch has not arrived.' I asked him why and he said, 'I believe naan takes longer to cook than rice.'

I asked him, 'So why didn't they tell me this? I would have changed my order.'

My assistant looked befuddled so I asked to speak to the production manager. There was no one around. I looked for the driver – he wasn't there. You must keep in mind that it was terribly hot and I was hungry. I am really not my best in such circumstances.

I decided, if they couldn't feed me, so what? I have been feeding myself all these years, haven't I? Off I went in a huff and bought myself lunch at the hotel. I waited in my costume for the next five hours just in case they needed me. They said they would call me, you see.

Finally, at about six, I called the production manager and reminded him that I was getting delayed for my flight, and asked if I could leave. He responded in a few minutes, saying, yes, I could go.

I got a boor of a driver.

Even though I can handle most boors, this one took the cake. I was faintly scared by his attitude. He was storming about, tossing my suitcase into the boot, slamming the door and frowning. And then, to top it all, he drove like a maniac. *This* was the guy I was going to be alone with for the next hour and a half? No way! When I asked him to stop the car he didn't. He actually ignored me. So I scared him right back by opening the door while the car was moving. The foolish man thought the dumb actress was going to jump and screeched to a halt. I had no such intention and stepped out of the car haughtily.

By now I was feeling a little low. They mess up my lunch, make me wait unnecessarily for five hours, send me this chappie *and* I am probably late for my flight.

Nevertheless, I gritted my teeth, hopped into another car and arrived at the airport well in time for my flight. Some solace. I strolled across to the airline counter and the lady there smiled sweetly at me and said, 'I am sorry, ma'am, this is a cancelled ticket.'

That did it. I had told them again and again that there was a shoot the next day and I simply had to be in Madras and they gave me a cancelled ticket? I was hopping mad. But I had the presence of mind to first book a new ticket before calling not the production team but the director. The whole tamasha came to an end after many apologies from the director and general faffing by the production guy and sniffs and tears from the fool actress.

I boarded the flight and settled into my seat with a sigh. Except for a hijacking or a crash, nothing else could go wrong now. The captain started making his announcements. I wasn't really paying attention until he mentioned the airline's name. 'Kingeefisher...' he said. I smiled lightly and continued staring blankly. I heard it again and there was a... snort of laughter from the guy next to me. Soon all of us were laughing.

The guy across the aisle said, 'He's Portuguese, hence the accent.'

I replied, 'Ah, but it is really funny.'

The man leaned back and the one next to him leaned forward so he could see me.

'I am Portuguese too,' he said.

I decided to brazen it out. 'Oh, do say "kingfisher" for us!'

Amidst general laughter we took off. When it was time to land we all waited eagerly for the kingeefeesher announcement but an Indian pilot came on the air and we slumped back with a palpable air of disappointment.

Suddenly it occurred to us that the aircraft hadn't moved in the last ten minutes and the doors still hadn't opened.

The Portuguese guy quipped, 'The captain's saying, yeah, make fun of me now.'

Someone else said, 'We should go check if he is there at all.'

Another man across the aisle said, 'Maybe they don't know how to open the door.'

By now there was a small group of passengers around me eagerly bouncing ideas and starting to laugh.

I chimed in, 'Maybe the instructions were in English.'

The Portuguese man replied, 'Hey, three hours from now when you are roasting in this flight because you are still locked in, it's not going to matter what language it was written in.'

Another one chirped, 'Oh, look, they are getting the key

... So *this* is what they left behind in Hyderabad.'

We were all laughing now and people from the front of the aircraft were looking back almost wistfully at this group of merry travellers. My guffaw as usual topped the charts in terms of volume, with the guy behind me following at a close second. Finally, they managed to get the door open and our group – of complete strangers – happily trudged out of the plane. On the way out, the guy behind me said loudly to the airhostess, 'It was a *memorable* flight.' And we were in splits again.

As my laughter faded and I walked over to collect my luggage, I marvelled at how completely my mood had changed. From my usual energetic start I had transitioned to irritation, then fury, then tears and now here I was, laughing and joking with complete strangers whom I would most likely never see again.

It was as if all the seasons had been rolled into one day. I was quite grateful about the order of the seasons though. My summer's day had become winter but everything was all right now. The usual spring was back in my step as I walked out of the airport with a smile on my face.

Despite the swings in my moods, my workload was moving only in one direction and that was up. If early to bed and early to rise makes a man healthy, wealthy and wise, I was fast becoming a sick old fool! The number of night shoots had shot up dramatically and I had begun to dread going through yet

> **Note to self:** When things go wrong, as difficult as it may be, try to be open to the things that are going right.

another day where I felt like I had jet lag and my body felt like someone had used it as a punching bag.

But despite the complaints, I have always been fortunate enough to have amusing things happen to me during my trips to work. Is it because I am always ready for a good laugh or am I just surrounded by funny things? Either way I am grateful for these reprieves, for they gave me the energy to battle my reluctance and aversion to certain aspects of my work.

My assistant Vasanth, my driver Veeramani (the only one who can handle Anu Hasan's idiosyncratic insistence for punctuality) and I make a great team. When we travel together one of us always notices something funny and brings it to the notice of the other two. This results in all three of us chuckling happily. One evening when we had almost reached the shooting location we got stuck at a railway signal.

Now I have been brought up with a healthy respect for personal safety (contrary to public opinion when I hosted *Anu Alavum Bhayam Illai*) and I was reluctant to cross the train tracks when the barrier was down. Veeramani said he would go and find out when the gate would open. Meanwhile, I received a call from the director saying everyone else was at the spot and ready, so I reluctantly braced myself to walk cross the tracks. (Another one of my idiosyncracies is that I hate to make anyone wait – even if *they* are early and I am on time, although in this case I was the one who was getting late.)

Vasanth collected my make-up kit while I got out of the car and we both started strolling towards the gate. Veeramani had almost reached it. When he was about three feet away, the gate opened suddenly. What happened after that made us laugh for a good few minutes.

When Veeramani saw the gate open, he turned around yelling, 'Aiyyo, ma'am ... ma'am...' and started running towards me. I took one look at him and said, 'Aiyyaiyyo!' and ran towards the car. Vasanth saw me running and ran to the car as well. We all jumped in and began to laugh as we shot across the level crossing.

As we went past the gate on the other side, we met one of the production guys who started running alongside the car and asked us, 'What happened? What happened?' Then he noticed all of us laughing and fell back with a bewildered look on his face. We continued laughing until we reached the sets.

All through that night, whenever I felt my enthusiasm flagging under the stress and tension, I retrieved this incident from my memory and felt myself lighten up at once. I narrated it to a few people on the sets and laughed all over again. I must confess that no one else seemed to find it funny, or at least as funny as I did, but that's because they didn't have the visual I had.

There have been several other incidents – like when I looked at the policeman who stopped my car so that pedestrians could cross and I gasped at his sudden appearance only to have him gasp right back at me either because he recognized me or was mocking my gasp. Or the time we saw a man wildly windmilling his arms as he stood on the divider on Mount Road. Or when I had asked Vasanth to remind me to buy a new washbasin and he mumbled out the reminder at one in the morning on our way back from shoot. Each of these incidents made me laugh. I think the three of us looked forward to that if nothing else in our day.

I loved the happy smiles we shared when I got into the car and I loved the tongue-in-cheek remarks Vasanth made and Veeramani's delighted chuckle which prompted him to grab the steering wheel tightly in order to keep the car on course. But most of all, I loved the sound of our laughter filling the small car, laughter shared between three strangers who would walk together for only one part of our lives. And each time I crawled out of the car and walked across to my door on aching feet, I would tell them both to drive home safely. For if nothing else, I looked forward to our next trip where we could all laugh together again... What an unlikely team we made: an assistant, a driver and a sick old fool!

Years have passed and in that time Veeramani is no longer in touch with me, I am no longer the host of *Koffee with Anu* and Vasanth is reportedly in jail for murder. (Yes, you heard me right!)

I used to hang on to the moments of happiness to help me get through the difficult phases, repeating to myself my father's favourite quote: 'This too shall pass.' It was only later that I realized he applied it to the happy moments as well.

When I look back at the path my so-called career has taken, I marvel at the chance occurrences that led me to it. 'If' is the word that changes it all, don't you agree?

> **Note to self:** This too shall pass.

It all started with me agreeing to do *Indira* on a whim and my on-and-off love affair with the camera has been on for nearly twenty years now.

For the past few years, I have had the luxury of choosing whom I work with. I have accepted projects solely on the strength of my liking for the director. I know most people are not able to make this kind of choice, which is all the more reason why I think I am fortunate.

This kind of approach is actually quite liberating. Before one of my trips to London, Periappa told me he would introduce me to a film-maker he knew in Liverpool. I completely forgot about it until months later I got an email from Joe Eshwar, asking me if I would be willing to play a role in his multilingual film *Kunthapura*. When we spoke on the phone I took an instant liking to Joe.

He said he wanted me to play the role of Gowri Iyer, a TV journalist. When I expressed my reservations about speaking Malayalam he said I would mainly be speaking in English in front of the TV camera and in any case my character was from Palakkad so my Malayalam accent would be excused. His confidence gave me the courage to say yes. The fact that Periappa (Charu Hasan) was also playing a role in the film meant I would finally get to work with the one Hasan brother I hadn't worked with.

I thought this would be one of those instances when people ask you to be part of a project and then nothing comes out of it. Believe me, in this industry that is more often than not the case.

But I was wrong. Several months later, when I was filming for a Telugu film in Hyderabad, I got a call from Joe asking me if I could film for him for a few days. And the days he wanted perfectly matched with the days I had planned on lazing and catching up with friends.

I agreed to give up my lazing time and the *Kunthapura* journey began. I landed in Bangalore where I was met by Achaayan and a friend of his who was an officer in Air Traffic Control. If you asked me what role Achaayan plays, my answer would be: 'I'm not quite sure.' Was he one of the producers? A mentor? An actor? A friend of Joe's? I didn't know. Later I discovered that he was all that and more.

Joe has this ability to draw people into helping him. Bangalore traffic being what it is, we were hours away from the location of the shoot. Light was fading fast and Joe was fretting about not being able to film. We stopped at a village for tea and out of the blue a villager, who heard Joe lamenting, came forward to ask what the problem was. When he heard we needed a location to film, he took Joe over to a piece of land he owned and offered to allow us to film there. It suited Joe perfectly. Joe tells me he has encountered this attitude throughout his journey and that without all the help from unexpected quarters, he would never have been able to complete the movie.

Working with Joe's team was a refreshing change. To a man, everyone was excited about the film. Biyon the protagonist was young, dedicated and enthusiastic. They all looked at me a little cautiously when I landed, as the weight of my surname tends to instil in most people a misplaced sense of awe. But once they realize how different I am from the other stars in the family – basically, that I am NOT one – the wariness is replaced by warmth. It was no different in *Kunthapura*.

I am not being arrogant when I say that I am competent

before the camera. Talking to the camera is something I have done a lot and, as Gowri Iyer (the character I played), I'd like to think I did my reporting bits fluidly. It earned me their respect. Combined with the warmth of our interaction, by the end of the first day, I was completely accepted into their team.

I also learnt that when you give an actor a safe environment you can get the best out of him or her. I saw this happen with Nanditha, a real-life reporter who was acting for the first time. Although she began nervously, when we gave her the time and reassured her, she delivered a performance completely different from the nervous person she started out as.

My journey in *Kunthapura* is not just comprised of moments of sincerity, gratitude, competence and chance encounters. My irrepressible sense of mischief generated memories too.

We were in two different cars on our way back from the shoot. Each car had a walkie-talkie so that we could communicate. Biyon decided he was going to entertain us and he started singing horribly off-tune songs. We suffered it for a while and then, at the first opportunity, I grabbed the walkie-talkie from Joe and said in a disguised voice, 'This is Inspector Bhavani. Who is this on official police frequency?'

There was pin-drop silence from Biyon in the other car while we all started grinning. I held the walkie-talkie out to the driver and told him to say the same thing in Kannada. After a few minutes a timid Biyon said, 'Hello?'

We controlled our laughter and I turned on the walkie-talkie and made static noises and ended with: 'Breaking the law. Please stop the car.'

By this time everyone in our car was laughing. There wasn't a peep from Biyon for the next ten minutes. Finally he said, 'Hello? I know this is not the police...' If he could have heard how tremulous his voice was, he would have known he was convincing no one.

We never let him hear the end of it. Even now when I think back to that incident, an involuntary smile spreads across my face. He still addresses me as Inspector Bhavani. At the end of the day, these are the memories that make every journey in life special.

I'd like to think I have gained friends from this project. And it was all based on chance occurrences. If Periappa hadn't mentioned Joe, I wouldn't have been as open to Joe's approach. If the dates hadn't fit in perfectly, I wouldn't have worked in the film. If I hadn't been made to feel welcome I wouldn't have felt as much of a sense of ownership as I did. If Joe hadn't been the kind of person he is, he would not have had such unstinting support from friends and strangers alike. And if we had not had such fun, the journey would not have sparkled as much.

> **Note to self:** 'If' is the word that changes it all. Coupling that with 'Why not' has resulted in some of the best experiences in my life.

DRIVE AND AMBITION

I think this is going to be the shortest chapter in the book. You see, drive is something I have in abundance – but I have very little ambition. I know that happiness is not linked to my bank account or the car I drive or the clothes I wear or the job I do. Of course the sense of security that a solid bank balance gives you is very nice indeed, but how much is enough?

When I was a child, one of the questions that teachers seemed to favour was: 'What is your ambition in life?' I remember – with a fair degree of pride – answering, 'To be happy.' It is only now that I appreciate what a wonderful approach to life that is. Over the years I have seen many people chase their dreams while missing important milestones in life and I have wondered how happy they were.

In school, my teachers were of the opinion that if I reduced my involvement in sports and extra-curricular activities, I would get a state rank in my board exams. Obviously they didn't know that the way I interpreted that comment meant that I did exactly what they *didn't* want me to. The fact that they thought I was capable was good enough for me. I felt as if I had achieved it. So while

I continued with basketball, athletics, quizzes, etc., I also worked hard at getting a good rank but at no point was I aiming for a state rank.

Consider *Koffee with Anu*. This was the celebrity talk show that I hosted for about four years. I am told this was the most successful talk show in Tamil Nadu. But I never set out to make it a success. I simply set out to do the best damned job I could.

Before every shoot, I spent time looking at the research given to me and scripting the whole thing in my mind. But things never go exactly according to plan and what I hoped to achieve was a rough sort of structure with enough freedom for the guests to explore new avenues if they wished. While I allowed them to meander, every now and then I would gently bring them back to the framework I had in my head and after a few tries I found the smoothest way of making this happen in any situation.

Since I hadn't set out to be the star of the show, I always took the approach of highlighting the guests' achievements and showing them in the best light possible, even if it meant exposing my ignorance. I never tried to corner them or put them in situations that would make them squirm. While I was busy doing this, what I didn't realize was that Brand Anu Hasan was being built. And suddenly 'Koffee' to most people meant 'Anu'.

The fact that I was now a household name didn't change my approach. I still got nervous and nauseous before

> **Note to self:** Fame and success are by-products of hard work and dedication. Long after the fame has faded, the satisfaction of a job well done will continue to shine.

every shoot, I was intensely focused on making the guest appear in the best light possible and I was still the same girl next door at heart. But it definitely delighted me when people complimented me for a job well done.

Which is why I discontinued the show.

While we were struggling to keep it a show on personal profiles, a particular clique in the channel felt we should use the show as a movie promo. Simply put, a movie promo is where everyone who has worked on the movie comes on the show to tell us how wonderful and different their movie is. And while they might be telling the truth in some cases, I felt that doing movie promos would make us lose the audience base we had built up. In my opinion, the fact that it was a casual open-ended chat show was what made *Koffee with Anu* work. Perhaps I was wrong. As pressure increased to do more movie promos, I tried to oblige. To be honest, I think I fell flat on my face. The role that was demanded of me now was that of a film aficionado, someone I couldn't aspire to be in a million years. I consider myself a people's person.

Knowing I wasn't doing a good job meant that I was reluctant to do more than a few promos in a month. The same clique came up with the idea of hosting parallel shows titled *Koffee with* 'someone else' while we continued *Koffee with Anu*. I was mildly offended but I could see what they were doing. *Koffee with Anu* was popular. They wanted to do movie promos. Anu was refusing. So let's do the movie promo with someone who is willing. I objected without expecting them to change their mind. We continued and I report with glee that they didn't have much success trying to establish that particular route.

When we were going to renew the contract for season four, I wanted an assurance that they wouldn't do *Koffee*-with-someone-else simultaneously. The channel was vague. And then they did the one thing that made my hackles rise. They got in Shruti (my cousin who had jus done a movie in Tamil) and filmed a *Koffee* shoot with someone else as the host. I had had enough. My email to the channel head was to the point and succinct. I explained how I thought they were diluting the Koffee brand that had been built but I understood that it was important for them to do movie promos and generate revenue. Despite the fact that I hadn't yet signed on the dotted line for the next season, I flew down and finished filming the scheduled episodes.

Most people thought I was being stupid. They thought if I hung around and reached a compromise, I would be the next Oprah Winfrey of India. They were making the same mistake my teachers made at school. I felt as if I had already won.

But to be fair, I have no ambition to be anyone else but me and that's good enough.

Note to self: When you define success as a job well done, accepting your limitations becomes that much more important. The sooner you identify them the happier you will be.

I'd like to think that I continue to have the clarity I had as a child – that my ambition in life is to be happy. And my determination to give complete focus to whatever I am doing at that moment has meant that I do rather well at most things. What I lack in skill and technique I make up for with sheer perseverance and pig-headedness.

When it comes to life, saying 'Yes

I can' is a great attitude. Or so I have always thought. And once I have told myself I can do it, it is extremely unusual for me to give up.

Case in point: last week. I had just finished shooting for the day and it was already 7 p.m. Returning home meant a forty-five-minute tube ride to London Bridge and then another train to get home. The train I needed to get on was the 8.04 from London Bridge. My tube would reach at 7.56 which gave me about seven minutes to hop on. Too precise? Well, you have to be because the public transport system in London is almost always on time, sometimes irritatingly so.

As the tube rolled in I looked at the time: 7.56 exactly. I had three flights of escalators to cross before I could make it to the platform, that too with a make-up kit and a suitcase. As I stepped out of the tube hoisting my luggage, I wondered if I could make it. Almost immediately, a voice inside my head said 'Yes, I can'. So I lunged out of the tube and launched, myself onto the first escalator.

The funny thing about the UK is that on the roads you overtake from the right but when you are on the escalator, people stand on the right and the ones who want to make an intrepid dash for the top keep to the left. So did I. This escalator had about forty-odd steps and I trotted up briskly, reaching the top only slightly out of breath.

Seven-fifty-seven and a few seconds, said my mental clock, which I must tell you, is fairly accurate most of the time. I half-walked-half-jogged across to the next flight of escalators. Another forty steps. This wasn't going to be as easy as the first one. After all, I am no featherweight and I was carrying luggage too. By the time I reached the top of this one, I was panting rather heavily and loath to admit that my legs felt a tad weak. Ahead of me was the ticket barrier and I decided to use the time to take deep breaths to regulate my breathing as I walked up to it. Seven-fifty-eight and forty seconds, said my mental clock.

After what must have looked quite a comical struggle as I held my luggage in one hand and hunted for my ticket inside a coat pocket that suddenly seemed too deep, I shuffled through the ticket barrier, half expecting to get whacked on the hip by the closing barrier. But before I could enjoy the relief that this didn't happen, my mental clock chimed eight.

One more flight of escalators, I thought tiredly. I couldn't run up but...? Yes, I could. So I set off. After a few steps I realized I was too tired and decided to wait this one out. After all, I still had three minutes.

When the escalator reached the top it was 8.01. I glanced at the display board and saw that the 8.04 was indeed on time and was leaving from platform four. I turned towards platform four and stopped short in dismay. I had forgotten about the inclined passage that led up to the platform. I should have saved some of my energy for a contingency like this. Then I could have drawn from my reserves, just like I do in life. And here I was scraping the bottom. (I must confess that there have been moments in life when I have been in similar spots.) I was close to giving up. I couldn't possibly run up this passage, hauling my stuff, I just couldn't. Just then a passenger jogged past me and the stupid voice inside my head said, 'Yes, I can' and I started clumsily struggling up the slope. Halfway through I heard the familiar rumbling that signalled the arrival of the train and I tried in vain to increase my pace.

8.02 and fifty seconds.

The doors closed thirty seconds before departure so I really had to hurry if I wanted to get on that train. By now my breath was coming in loud rasps and I was feeling distinctly weak. As I emerged dishevelled onto the platform I saw that the carriage was a good thirty metres away. I had about forty seconds before the doors closed. 'Yes, I can,' said that stubborn voice again and I lurched forward. The guard whistled, urging people to climb in quickly, which gave rise to a surge of panic that sent me stumbling a little faster towards the train.

I clambered aboard with seconds to spare. Panting heavily, I sent a message to Graham: 'Made it on the 8.04.' I felt ill and I actually thought I was going to faint. I leaned weakly against my seat in the crowded train and waited for the sense of triumph that never came.

Instead, another voice said, 'Yes, you made it. But did you have to?'

I could have slapped myself. After thumping that voice for not having spoken up earlier! Surely it could have asked that question before I half-killed myself? At this point I would like to add that anyone who says, 'Yes, it could but did it have to?' is also in danger of being thumped!

> **Note to self:** I still think saying 'Yes, I can' is a good attitude to have. But now I think I shall remember to tag to it the question: 'Do I have to?'

LOOKING FOR THE
SUNNY SIDE

While growing old is inevitable, growing up is an option. How wonderful that particular truth is. I am often accused of looking at the world through distinctly rose-tinted glasses. If ever there was a candidate susceptible to cynicism, it ought to be me. But oddly enough, I am not cynical.

Maybe it is because I make a conscious effort to keep cynicism at bay, or maybe it's in my genetic makeup. I don't know and I really don't care. I find joy in the simple things in life and go about looking for the same pleasures that gave me happiness as a child.

It is not surprising that in the hustle-bustle of everyday, we lose sight of those very things that were once attainable and focus instead on the elusive prize that we assume will give us happiness. I can hear a collective groan as I don my philosopher's hat so I shall quickly take you all to my favourite getaway – Mudaliar Kuppam.

This is a water sports centre run by Tamil Nadu Tourism Development Corporation. It is an hour and a half away from Madras and is a place where I have spent many a happy hour canoeing, riding a water scooter and having solo picnics.

Perumal is one of the guys who work there. I am quite fond of this pleasant cheerful man who has never verbalized his curiosity about an adult female making solo trips in her Scorpio to canoe and drive the water scooter. He always welcomes me with a smile. That day, though, I had a friend with me. As usual, I asked Perumal, 'What shall we do different today?' He knew me well enough by now to understand that I already had the answer. He waited, smiling patiently. 'Why don't you drop us off to the beach on the other side?' I suggested. He nodded and went off to bring the water scooter closer to the docks.

We hopped on and Perumal took off at high speed with a casual confidence that never fails to reassure me. (Although I admit I do lay a tentative hand on his shoulder to brace myself at the start.) The feel of the wind on our faces and the way the vehicle smoothly skimmed over the water at 80 kilometres an hour brought an involuntary smile to my face and I yelled over my shoulder, above the noise of the wind, 'Isn't this mindblowing?' My friend must have agreed – the wind was too loud and I was too busy lapping up the exhilaration of the moment to hear.

Perumal dropped us off at the shore and promised to return for us in a few hours. I shrugged off the life jacket I was wearing and made for the beach. There wasn't a soul in sight. And apart from the rush of waves and the wind whispering in the trees, there was no sound. I shot a smile at my friend and bounded ahead. There is something so brilliantly liberating about being the only people for as far as your eyes can see.

My friend was lost in thought and I wandered around aimlessly. I stood for a while where the waves frothed, trying to see how deep my feet would get buried if I stood without moving. After facing about twenty waves, I was only ankle deep so I gave up. I had a sudden inspiration as I drew back from the waves. I got down on my knees and started building a sand *gopuram*. It had been decades since I had last built one and I was delighted as the techniques came back to me. Not content with a temple, I built a lingam. Then I scrounged around for driftwood and gave the lingam the customary three stripes, located a wild berry and stuck it in the middle. After an hour and a half I sat back and surveyed my handiwork with satisfaction.

My friend strolled up to me and said, 'Not bad for a non-believer. Except the *pattai* is on the wrong side.'

I was about to argue with him and then realized the mistake and cheerfully corrected it. Then I said in satisfaction, 'Beautiful, no? Look out for the headlines tomorrow. *Mysterious appearance of lingam in abandoned beach.* The next thing you know, they've built a temple here. When you see that temple, remember *I* am that mysterious force!'

I threw a delighted smile at my friend, who shook his head and looked at me. I knew exactly what he was thinking. It's never too late to be a teenager!

What's age got to do with it? No one cares anyway and your responsibilities will still be waiting when you revert to your usual self.

Note to self:
Sometimes it is
important to forget
to be your age.

Which is one of the reasons why I play basketball despite being well over the 'acceptable' age. How often do you see a motley group of women aged between twenty and forty-five gathered at the basketball court? Quite often, if you consider our group. We used to play either in the corporation grounds at Nandanam or at Stella Maris College. I have had many wonderful moments playing with my team. One day, when I was playing at Stella Maris, someone asked my teammate, 'Which batch do you belong to?' She responded with her year of passing. Curious eyes turned to me and they looked back at her and continued, 'And Anu belongs to...?' Another teammate chimed in, 'She belongs to us.' We all laughed and continued with our warm-ups. And it's true, I do feel a sense of belonging when I play with them.

Over the years, each woman has come up with a regime that works best for her. Some sprint around the court, others stretch sedately on the side. A few practise shooting. Family pressures are forgotten, professional worries are left behind. A pleasant chatter echoes through the court punctuated by the rhythmic thud of the ball against the board or bouncing on the ground. Coach whistles and everyone stops what they are doing and obediently troops to the centre of the court, some of them asking, 'Who-who, coach?', asking him how he is going to divide the teams.

It is quite a pleasure to see the energy and enthusiasm everyone has for the game. Basketball always has this ability to draw people together. As I duck and dive and jump for rebounds, I forget we are no longer children. I go back to my college days when I used to be faster, my movements more economical. But playing basketball is like riding a cycle. Your mind never forgets the moves. It just takes longer to complete a move now.

One of the women flicks her wrist and I lunge forward. The ball ricochets off my extended hand and whizzes towards my teammate. I turn my head just in time to see her grab the ball and take aim. I whip around and start sprinting towards the ring, hoping to be there in time for the rebound. With a neat swish, the ball sinks into the net. A cheer goes up from both sides. It is our love for the game that drives us. Not the competition.

After about thirty minutes I am tired – I think age has caught up with me. But they tell me that I have expended my energy unnecessarily. Doing too many things at once, Coach says. 'You can't go for the rebound, cover your man, cut in for a pass and play defence all at the same time. At least not until you have built your stamina. You move around too much doing too many things.'

It occurs to me that I play basketball the way I live my life – stretching my limits, pushing my capabilities, handling several things at once. It's a good thing I play basketball well. And it's an even better thing that I have the stamina I need for living my life the way I want.

I am of the opinion that in these times of rushed meals, instant gratification and work pressures, it is all the more important to find time

> **Note to self:** Make allowances for your age but not too much lest you miss out on things you could have done if only you had made a little more effort.

for small pleasures. I am programmed to identify such things and that, I believe, is one of the reasons why people think I am happy most of the time. They are not wrong.

I do seem to find many opportunities that make me happy or at least make me smile. Who would think one would find reason to smile on Christmas Eve in Madras, when the streets were crawling with party-goers? Despite the fact that it's the season for goodwill, that Christmas there were an unusual number of boors on the roads. Poor driving was the least of the offences I can recollect.

I was driving home, surprisingly unaffected by the rude group of men in the next car leering at me. I passed a man selling huge colourful balloons on the roadside. In an instant I was transported back to my childhood when my dad once asked me, 'What would you do if you had one lakh rupees?' and I replied, 'Buy lots of balloons.' It gave me an insight into a child's mind and reminded me of a definition of what happiness really can be.

Somewhere along the line, I lost that insight for a while. If I had been chasing dreams, maybe I could have forgiven myself. But there are no excuses. I simply joined millions of others who completely lost their priorities in life. So, is buying a balloon a priority? Well, in a way, yes. So many days spent chasing deadlines instead of dreams, so many hours spent looking at a balance sheet of assets instead of a balance sheet of happiness. Life is really simple if you make it, is it not? Or maybe I am in a simplistic mood tonight. And I think that buying balloons signifies the beginning of an era for me. An era where I stop to … smell the balloons?

That evening I stopped the car, switched on my hazard lights like the conscientious driver that I am, and waved to the balloon-seller. He jogged across to my car. I asked for white balloons but he didn't have any. He had transparent ones and when I shook my head he looked so crestfallen I didn't have the heart to drive away without buying some.

So I gave him hundred rupees and carted home five big fat balloons.

It caused considerable amusement in my apartment complex. The watchman on night duty grinned at me and said, 'Merry Christmas.' I grinned back unabashedly. A neighbour, whom I've never spoken to, stopped on her way out and said, 'I see you like balloons.' I was tempted to say, 'Yeah, Einstein,' but it's the season of goodwill, remember? So she too received the unabashed grin.

I rang the doorbell. When my mum opened the door I thrust the balloons at her and yelled out, 'Merry Christmas!' My cat took one look at me, abandoned all ideas of giving me a warm welcome and raced across the slippery mosaic, slid around a corner, slammed into a wall, bounced off it and disappeared into a room. My mother looked as if she was tempted to do the same, but she smiled and let me into the house.

> **Note to self:**
> Remember to buy balloons/ flowers for yourself every now and then.

My father merely remarked, 'I see you have one lakh rupees.'

I have found that when you consciously start looking for the silver lining, after some time triggers start popping up automatically and you experience more than the average number of snatched moments of happiness. As a result you end up handling inconvenient situations with lower levels of frustration.

The rains in 2008 in Madras must have caused misery to most of the people in the city. The roads were flooded with water up to about a metre in some places. Everyone was advised to stay at home but as soon as the water levels started dropping there was one person who was walking around with a silly grin plastered on her face – yep! Me. My mother warned me that I was in danger of getting lynched if I was so obvious in my delight.

That morning, when it was time for me to leave for my workout, I realized the water stagnating outside my apartment was knee deep. I rolled up my trousers and gleefully splashed across the street. A rain-soaked man miserably pushed his bike past me. Out of consideration for his state, I schooled my expression into a slightly less happy one and held it until he had gone ahead. Then I climbed into my Scorpio and drove down to YMCA. Naturally it was deserted. I started my jog and realized I could do only two-thirds of the circuit as the rest was submerged. I wished I had brought my camera. The football field looked like a lake. I bet if I showed that picture to people and asked them to identify it they would have said it was Pulicat Lake or something.

When I came back to the main building to do my strength-training exercises I saw all the trainers trooping out with a ladder. I hurried behind them, not wanting to be left out of all the fun. They were going to climb the roof. I was almost bouncing up and down as I asked my trainer, 'Can I come too?'

'Do you want to go up as well, ma'am?' one of them asked me. Catch me saying no!

So there I was, climbing up to the roof on a rickety ladder, to check what was causing the water seepage down below. As one of my friends remarked later, 'Your only qualification was that you could climb that ladder.'

Being on the roof was a whole new experience. I found myself looking at a place I had been working out in for five years from a new vantage point. How lush and green the shrubs looked from above. Freshly bathed green is a glorious colour, have you ever noticed? Everything seemed different. The running track, the seemingly endless expanse of trees, the roof of the gym, the astro turf – things I see every day but they looked so different from up here.

It's just like life, I thought. You look at a situation or a person from a particular perspective and then suddenly you realize there is a facet you have missed out on. As I stood there absorbing the view, a movement caught my eye and I turned. Down below, near the trees, were two deer – a momma deer and baby deer. They were idly munching grass, oblivious to our presence. We were able to watch them unobserved for a good five minutes before momma looked up and stared straight at us. It was a strange feeling, as though we had been caught peeping. Baby looked at his momma and then turned his head to see what she was looking at. When he saw us standing on the roof and watching him, he bolted for the trees. Momma continued to stare at us unblinkingly for several seconds and then with cool arrogance she turned and sauntered off into the cover.

I laughed in delight and told my trainer, 'What a glorious

> **Note to self:** If you
> are open to it, you
> will always discover
> the unexpected.
> But you must be
> prepared to climb
> the ladder of
> detachment.

experience! Thank you for letting me climb up!'

My trainer smiled at me and said, 'You only did what you wanted to, ma'am.'

How true! But I never expected to experience what I just did – a new perspective and a display of attitude.

It started raining again on my way back. I was still grinning when a car drove past me, sending a wave across the bonnet of my Scorpio. I burst out laughing and as I turned my head, I caught the eye of two people who were watching me in bewilderment.

I waved at them merrily and continued driving my amphibian home. They wouldn't understand the joy of what I had experienced nor would they know that it would take more than a wave of muddy water to dampen my spirits that day. If I had the time – not to mention the courage – I would have tried to infuse them with my *joie de vivre*. but I don't suppose they were in the mood and it wasn't the best time for it either.

I thought about the deer and smiled again. The incident reminds me of an entirely different one. Here too an animal was involved.

Some breaks are planned to the last detail and some breaks just happen. This one belonged to the latter category.

Everyone in our family shares a love for Kodaikanal. My uncle owns a sizeable tract of land there (my grand uncle lives there and manages the land), My cousin has a lovely house in Kodai and I too have a piece of land there. It was this land that needed my attention. What was supposed to be a one-day trip to Kodai to sort out some details pertaining to my land turned into a four-day holiday trip.

My cousin had generously offered the use of her house while I was there and I happily accepted. She warned me to be careful, though. Apparently there were plenty of bison around that area and the occasional lone rogue bison was not unheard of. I had heard stories of them jumping fifty feet, tossing people around, and I had no intention of checking the validity of this firsthand.

The first day was uneventful, except for the four bars of chocolate and two packets of chips that I gorged on between lunch and dinner. But I decided that I could allow myself these holiday indulgences. I must mention, though, that I also spent the afternoon trudging up and down my land checking boundaries and am certain that I burned quite a few calories. My grand uncle accompanied me and on the whole it was a very peaceful day ... apart from his disdain when he found I didn't know which way north lay. Why on earth was it important for me to know which was north? Did he think we were wading through the Amazon jungle? He sniggered and made a wise crack about youngsters these days which I chose to ignore. He has always enjoyed getting me all riled up. The mischievous glint in his eyes gave him away but not before my temper flared. I always notice the grin on his face too late and realize that I have fallen into his trap yet again.

The next day, as expected, I woke up with a healthy dose of guilt as I remembered the chocolate bars and chips from the previous afternoon. So I set off on my own for a morning jog.

As I strolled down the driveway, I heard the girl from the next plot shout, 'Kaatu erumai!' Wild buffalo! I casually turned to look and found this huge fellow about a hundred feet away from me. I froze. All those stories about bison goring people flashed through my mind. I knew there wasn't a chance in hell of me outrunning him so I just stood there staring at him, not knowing what to do.

He looked at me for a few interminable seconds and then, with a disinterest that would have crushed me had it come from another human being, turned away and started ambling across the driveway. I waited a few more seconds before cautiously making my way towards the gate. Round one to the bison.

There was a general air of panic all around as the girl continued to yell and a little boy joined in the chorus, while a dog began to bark and run about aimlessly. That's when I heard the thundering of hooves. Without a second thought, I started running to the nearest gate even though I knew the gate was no obstacle to the dratted animal since it could scale higher walls. As I approached the gate and paused to look behind me, I caught a flash of black in the distance and realized that the silly creature had been running AWAY.

There was a man holding the gate open, urging me to enter. He said I was standing in the exact path that the bison usually took. I would have thought he was being kind if it weren't for the smirk on his face. He had seen me scramble madly. In order to bring him down a peg, I said, 'If the bison decided to, he could easily jump over this gate, right?' I watched maliciously as his smirk faded and pompously told him I was going in the opposite direction so maybe if I walked out now, the bison and I would go our separate ways. Sure, he said. As I began to walk, he said, 'It would be better if you went quickly.' That had me running out with more alacrity than grace. Round two to the man with the smirk.

Once I reached the road leading away from the golf course, I slowed down to a walk. As I determinedly continued walking away, throwing nervous glances over my shoulder every now and then, the chaos receded and faded into the distance. I walked for over an hour, garnering several curious looks. A woman striding purposefully down a road that led nowhere is bound to do that. Story of my life.

Having pacified my conscience about the chocolate and chips, I returned to the house to find the caretaker waiting for me. He asked me if I had had a good walk. I said yes, except for the bison, and narrated the incident. I confessed that I had been more than a little scared. He scoffed and said, 'You just had to tell him, "Ramachandra, po da," and he would have gone away.'

It raised a rather worrying point. What if the bison I met was NOT Ramachandra? If I called him by the wrong name wouldn't he get even more offended? You never know with these rogue bison. But I didn't tell him that. For all I knew, he'd come up with a list of names.

So I replied that I had been at a disadvantage since I didn't know Ramachandra by name and assured him that the next time I saw him, I would address him by his name and ask him to go away. Round three to the caretaker.

Can you visualize that? Me standing before a bison and saying, 'Ramachandra! Po da!'?

I smiled at the thought while the caretaker earnestly

began to explain that Ramachandra was a wild bison but he understood Tamil.

'That's nice,' I responded, distracted by the glorious smell of breakfast which the caretaker's wife's beckoned me to eat while it was still hot.

'They are sensitive creatures, you know. If you are affectionate towards them they are really quite gentle. They only wander in because they are curious about the cows and want some food and attention.'

I wasn't sure if he was talking about bison or men in general. (Okay okay, I take that back! I am ducking the punches aimed at me by all the lovely men – and women – in my life!)

Anyway, why am I telling you about this particular incident, you might ask. Well, this is, after all, about having fun and looking at the sunny side, isn't it? I could have focused on my fear, which was genuine, but I choose to focus on the ridiculousness of the situation – come on, admit it, Ramachandra made you smile!

But if you think I am the kind of person who always sees the sunny side of things, you couldn't be more wrong. I struggle. I give in to my anger and frustration before I manage to shrug aside the negativity and feel happy.

I remember a day, not so many years ago, when I seesawed between happiness and amusement, calm control and anger and frustration.

Two things made that day unique. One, my shoot got cancelled, and two, my dad was going to Thailand on film production related work. I decided to tag along. I love these impromptu trips. Of course, I had to work like a maniac in order to finish all my work for the four days that I was going to be away but that only meant I deserved the break.

The trip started off with a bang. When I reported at the airlines counter I was told that my name wasn't on the list. The girl at the counter was a trainee and I smiled at her encouragingly and said, 'I'm in no hurry. Take your time.' So confident was I that it was she who was making a mistake. She frantically pounded on some keys and then gave up and looked for assistance from a senior co-worker. He checked the database and then looked up and said, 'Ma'am, please don't use Makemytrip.com. We have been continuously facing such problems where the customer comes here and finds that his ticket has not been issued.'

I, still certain that I was right and everyone else was wrong, calmly dialled Makemytrip and was told, 'Sorry, ma'am, we have not been able to get you a ticket.'

A frisson of annoyance crept into my voice as I replied, 'But you charged my card, why didn't you tell me that I haven't got a ticket?'

'We will refund your card, ma'am,' came the disinterested reply.

I contemplated arguing with him but decided my priority was to get to Bangkok, not to fight with some lackey in the system. I asked the airlines official, 'Do you have a ticket I can book now?'

He looked at his system and nodded. 'Yes. But you have to go to the domestic terminal to collect it.'

'No problem,' I said. 'Could you please ask them to block it for me? I'll run across now.' I walked out of the terminal, chucked my laptop and suitcase onto a trolley and started jogging to the domestic terminal, happy to be burning a few calories. I'd missed my morning jog anyway.

I collected the ticket and jogged back. The officer at the counter said, 'We'll try and upgrade you to business class, ma'am.'

I paused. On the two previous occasions when this happened, I felt a thrill. But this time I felt guilty. I don't travel business class because it is too expensive. So when I get a free upgrade it means I am sitting amidst people who have paid through their nose while I haven't. I told myself that I would travel business class when I didn't feel guilty about spending so much money. Aloud I said, 'No, please don't. I have caused enough confusion as it is.'

The official looked surprised. 'You mean you *don't* want an upgrade?'

'Please don't take the trouble,' I said and, feeling very pleased with myself for having done the right thing, I walked off to immigration.

The first thing I did after immigration was call the lackey at Makemytrip.com and blast him and demand a refund. I said that if I found they had charged anything at all after the refund they would face a consumer court litigation. It felt good to growl, now that my trip was on track. I must add that my disillusionment with Makemytrip did not last and I continue to book my tickets using the site. I just make sure that my tickets have a PNR attached.

It was quite uneventful until I got into the plane. First, a couple of people came up to me during the flight and asked me who the next guests on *Koffee* were. A few more came up to chat with me. These incidents didn't bother me. But after lunch had been served and cleared away, and I was just beginning to doze off, I sensed a flash going off. I opened my eyes and saw some strange guy taking a picture of me. I looked at him and said please don't and he put away his camera. Of course he probably already had a charming picture of me with my mouth half open and my head lolling. I dozed off again. When I woke up next, the lady across the aisle told me that they had taken some more pictures. I was furious. I stomped up to the guy and told him, 'It's quite rude to take pictures of people without asking them. And what kind of culture taught you to take pictures when someone is sleeping?'

He probably didn't expect me to react in that way. He cowered and denied taking any pictures. Since I could hardly grab his camera and smash it – which was just what I wanted to do – I glared at him and stomped back to my seat. The rest of my flight was spent staring suspiciously at anyone who walked by me or paused before my row. Needless to say, it completely spoiled my flight.

Makes me wonder if I should have lived with the guilt of a free upgrade. Wait, I would have had to live with the guilt if I agreed to a free upgrade. Since I didn't, my enthusiastic photographer will have to live with a picture of me with my mouth open, head lolling. Hah! Good luck to him.

Note to self: A determined attempt to see the sunny side does not ensure that you will never lose sight of it. But it does ensure that you will notice it quicker once the clouds thin.

TRAVEL DIARY

There was a period in my life, between 2006 and 2009, when I was not bound to anything or anyone. What I loved most about this time was the freedom to take off and go where I liked whenever I felt like. Of course, I did have to plan my work schedule around it, but I had to plan little else.

When I was a child, we occasionally travelled to other countries but what I enjoyed most about travelling between 2006 and 2009 was that I travelled alone, taking a trip every July as a birthday present to myself. I took off for parts of the world unknown. So many places to go, so many things to do, so many people to meet. How do you fit it all into one life? Many people have a list of places they want to go to. I am not one of them. I don't have a list – I find them limiting; I want it all. I want to see every country in the world. Maybe I will, maybe I won't. But I have made some progress.

The first time it was Cambodia. It was like a dream come true. I had always spoken about Angkor Wat with hushed reverence. Never mind that I didn't bother brushing up on its history (neither before nor after my trip). To me, visiting a place is more about how it makes me feel. I don't feel the need to impress people with my knowledge. I am quite happy to expose my ignorance most of the time. But I digress.

I was in Singapore to compere a show and planned to make a detour to Cambodia on my way back. Imagine my delight when I found I could book a return trip from Singapore to Seam Reap for all of five thousand rupees. My frugal south Indian heart leapt in boundless joy. I quite enjoyed the disbelieving looks of the other people who were part of the show. 'You're going to spend your birthday alone in Cambodia?' was a common refrain and one I never tired of hearing.

I sang happy birthday to me and took off for Seam Reap. I knew I could get a visa on arrival. I had a moment of panic when I realized I didn't have a passport-sized photo on me but I managed to find one from the machine they had placed for travellers like me.

I was staying in a bed-and-breakfast called Mysteres d'Angkor run by two Frenchmen, Philippe and Pascal. I had booked my room online and we had exchanged quite a few chatty emails. Philippe had coached me earlier: 'Do not ask the driver if he has come from Mysteres d'Angkor. Ask him, "Where are you from?" This way you won't get cheated and taken to another hotel.' Used to learning dialogues, I was ready with my lines but was saved from having to deliver them since I saw a placard with my name as soon as I exited the airport.

I walked alongside the cheerful Soomna and stopped short in front of my transport – a rickshaw attached to a motorcycle. I promptly had him take a picture of me standing next to it. He chatted cheerfully on the way and considering he was looking over his shoulder to talk to me, it was a wonder we didn't have any encounters with lamp posts. He was curious about whether I had a boyfriend and why I hadn't brought him along. When the conversation took a personal turn I began to worry that perhaps I was being kidnapped. I wondered if single women with no boyfriends were more likely to be kidnapped than women who had boyfriends. I was quite relieved that we reached the hotel before I had convinced myself that I needed a boyfriend.

Given that I was paying only forty-two US dollars a night, the place was wonderful. Lots of greenery and despite the fact that their menu was limited, the food was excellent.

The next day I took Soomna and his rickshaw and zoomed off to Angkor Wat. It was beautiful. I had my camera with me and went berserk taking pictures. One of my favourite shots is what I call 'peacemaker colt'. There was a colt sitting in a lawn with a monument in the background. I was so impressed with the picture it made that I didn't notice that its mother was tied to a tree nearby. I was focused on getting the frame right and didn't see that I was too close to mama horse. Suddenly I heard a snuffle and turned my head in time to see her coming at me with bared teeth. I ran out of her reach and started laughing almost immediately at how funny it must have appeared to an onlooker. Still laughing, I came back and took the photograph I wanted. Since mama horse had gnashed her teeth at me I excluded her from my picture.

As I walked towards the entrance of the temple, along the Naga causeway, I almost felt as if I was in the

Thanjavur Brihadeeshwara temple. It seemed so familiar. The construction and architecture were only slightly different – the apsaras had sharper noses and slightly oriental eyes but other than that I could only see the similarities. I wandered about Angkor Wat and found a monument which had really steep steps. I don't know if you've seen them but these steps are only about half a foot wide, so you can't place your foot perpendicularly. You have only enough space to place your foot sideways – which means you have to climb in a zigzag manner.

With my backpack, I huffed and puffed up the steps, conscious of the fact that I was being watched by several shopkeepers. I thought they were impressed with my agility and it spurred me on. It was only when I got to the top, completely out of breath, that I realized that on the other side of the monument there were comfortable steps built exclusively for tourists like me, complete with handrails. Ah, well...

Note to self: If you enjoy the journey rather than the destination, it doesn't matter if you have made more of an effort to reach the top.

That first day I spent the better part of four hours walking around but I was conscious of the fact that I had Soomna waiting for me. So the next day, I hired a cycle and did the rounds of Angkor Thom and Preah Khan. I think I cycled over twenty-two kilometres that day.

It was a fantastic experience. It was raining and there was no one on the road and I could almost fool myself that I was all alone inside a forest. Each time a monument loomed before me, I would stop, get off my cycle, and wander around admiring the structures. Preah Khan was an amazing experience. You can see nature reclaiming what is hers. Huge trees seem to swallow entire walls. I couldn't get over the fact that there was such a striking resemblance to our architecture in a temple complex constructed 900 years ago in another country.

I think this was the best birthday I've ever had. I bought things that were completely useless, bargained shamelessly and generally behaved like a tourist. I ate whatever food was available and thanked my parents for having brought me up as a non-vegetarian. Vegetarians have a rather limited choice in Cambodia. You can eat bok choy with carrots, bok choy with beans or bok choy with bok choy.

I know I will go back to Cambodia, and this time I will visit all the other monuments that I couldn't see. I wonder how many trips it will take for me to cover all two hundred acres of the temple complex. All said and done, Cambodia is a dream.

After I returned from this trip, I was hooked onto the idea of solo travel. But since I didn't have a list of must-see places, I spread the world map before me, positioning it so I knew where Europe and Asia were, closed my eyes and put my finger on the map. Wherever my finger landed, I went.

The first time it was Romania. My finger landed a little to the left of Romania but I nudged it to Romania. All my plans were confirmed and paid for before I left India and included everything I wanted to do on my own. I remember booking myself into a remote bed-and-breakfast in a place called Brasov (or was it Rasnov?), a few hours from Bucharest. Parts of Eastern Europe had a shady reputation and I was told to watch out in particular for cab drivers in Bucharest. So on my way to the train station from the airport, I pretended to know the route, using what I'd read up on the internet to bolster that impression. I imagine the cabbie was fooled, since I reached the station unharmed. My holiday was filled with walks and treks and delicious Romanian food prepared by the hosts.

I visited Cyprus the next year. This time I was a bit more adventurous. I got myself an international driving licence, hired a car from the airport and drove myself. I spent two days at a villa near Tochni and then three days at a bed-and-breakfast called Limos Inn at Lofou. I remember stopping the car just off the highway and walking down to a deserted dam. There wasn't a soul in sight and I wandered about until the sun got too strong. Then I trekked back, weaving my way through shrubs and rocky slopes, and drove back to the bed-and-breakfast. Later, I was told that the area I had been walking in harboured a lot of rattlesnakes. Since I hadn't encountered any, I shrugged the information off. Would I still have explored those slopes if I had known about the rattlesnakes? I probably would have, but shhhhh, don't tell my mother that!

In 2009 it was Austria. The reason I chose it was as random as the previous ones. On one of my trips to the US, I'd met a lady who lived in Vienna. She was a tap dancer. I met her about four years ago and we had been in touch through email ever since. So I thought, why not visit Austria?

I landed in Vienna to brisk sunshine and my adventure started almost immediately. I could have taken the taxi to

my hotel but it seemed too tame. So, armed with directions
from the internet, I set off in search of the CAT – City Airport
Train. I must have looked confident because a Hungarian
walked up to me and asked me to help him buy a ticket for
the CAT, which I did obligingly. Little did he know that he
was my guinea pig. Once the experiment was a success, I
went about buying my own ticket. We travelled to the city
centre together, chatting idly. As we reached our destination,
I felt that he was getting a bit too friendly, so I politely
turned down his offer of 'coffee' and strode off towards the
U Bahn. I had to take the U4 to a station called Shottentor
and then the U2 to Shottentor Universitat, then the tram to
Wattgasse. Everything went well and I landed in Wattgasse
and walked up to my little hotel. Little is the right word for
the hotel. But the right word for my room is 'tiny'. But I was
only spending one night there so it hardly made a difference.
The next day I was leaving for a place called St Georgen am
Reith. (And no, it was not where *The Sound of Music* was
filmed but I think it is where I would shoot a film if I ever
muster the courage to do so.)

Wandering around in Europe is delightful; I wandered
around Vienna the whole of the next day. I felt completely
safe simply because I was ignored. No one stared at me
because they knew me. No one stared at me because I was
taller or bigger. They simply went about their business,
except for two Italian admirers who began to follow me,
clutching their heart and pretending to swoon. I laughed
but gently turned down their offer to buy me dinner. They
left looking suitably distressed – until they found another
woman they could try their theatrical skills on.

Friendly women in cafes chatted with me – although one conversation I had was a little strange. A woman spoke to me about how she had spoken to God and he had said that there were two children in Tibet who were in need of her and she was going to India to find them. Good luck with that. Another woman commented on how unusual it was to see a woman from India travelling on her own. I like unusual. Unless she meant 'strange'.

As for the men, well, I knew that not everyone was going to be as amusing as my dear Italian Lotharios, so I was fairly careful about making eye contact. I escaped to the countryside unscathed.

This was supposed to be a simple journey consisting of two train changes. But since the railway tracks were being repaired, it ended up being a journey consisting of one train, two bus trips, and then the two train changes. I was lucky to find a helpful young man who happened to be a film-maker of all things! If it weren't for him, I would have been waiting until today in a place called Waidhoffen for a train that would never come.

The hunting castle where I stayed was beautiful although I was a little disturbed about having to walk down long unlit corridors that had hunting trophies mounted on the walls. Made me wonder, do stags and elks and chamois have ghosts? What about boars? Were the corridors haunted?

If I was possessed by an elk ghost would I prance around goring people?

I fell in love with the countryside. I rented a bicycle and cycled (on the wrong side of the road) and explored. There is something magical about grey asphalt snaking before you with lush green mountains on either side, the gradient occasionally broken by the gurgling water of the Ybbs (pronounced eebs).

On one of my cycling trips, I saw a roped enclosure of happy-looking cows and immediately clambered off my cycle to take pictures. I stepped closer to the enclosure when I was distracted by a calf standing all by himself a few feet away inside the enclosure. He was so beautiful that I turned to capture him on my camera. In trying to do so, I had to step away from the enclosure since he was edging towards his mother who stood next to the rope. I had just got the perfect frame of mommy and calf when he brushed against the rope and yowled loudly and sprinted away. The rope was electrified! I almost dropped the camera. Thankfully he was unharmed. The calf looked at me reproachfully and I couldn't resist taking another picture of him, laughing as I did so. My landlady later told me that one could actually hold the rope and only get a slightly unpleasant feeling and that it wasn't all that dangerous – but I was thankful that I had not got into my head to get a close-up of the happy cows and tried to climb into the roped enclosure myself. The calf would have been the one laughing then!

I met my friend Astrid in Vienna and we visited places that are kept secret from tourists and gorged on the most delicious apricot dumplings. I strolled along Naschtmarkt

Note to self: When planning a trip, your itinerary should include what you want to see and not what others think you should see. So what if you have been to Agra and not seen the Taj Mahal? (Been there done that – not seen the Taj.)

in Vienna but refused to take pictures of the colourful stalls, much to the disappointment of Mr Werner, Astrid's husband. I'd much rather take shots of unexplored beauty than the usual crowded tourist spots. However, to humour him, I took one picture near a vegetable stall. But I stoically refused to see Salzburg and Innsbruck. My trip, my terms.

My holiday in the Austrian countryside was filled with bicycle rides, lazy lunches, walks, happy cows, reproachful calves and solitude. I did want to go on a moonlit ride up a hill but that would be pushing my luck. Travelling on my own doesn't mean I let common sense fly away in the face of impulse. When I look back on these solo trips, I can see the fun I have had, the chances I have taken and the lessons I have learnt.

Travelling alone is great – you do everything at your own pace and you do whatever you want to do. But on the flipside, especially if you are a woman, you need to be a little cautious about where you stay and how you plan on getting there.

For instance, I always chose flights that landed mid-morning, my logic being that the chance of getting mugged or something worse is slightly lower when the day has just started. When it came to accommodation, I checked reviews from multiple websites before deciding on one, and I always made sure I had an email confirming what I had paid and what was due. And finally, I always picked up a local sim card and called my parents to let them know that I had landed and where I could be contacted.

As you can see, my concept of travelling solo was a nice blend of caution and adventure.

But my holidays haven't always been abroad and they haven't always been to places I have never been to before. I also revisit some places. Goa is one of them.

> **Note to self:**
> Travelling solo can be a lot of fun but only if you pay heed to the rules of personal safety.

You don't have to bother making an itinerary for Goa. The last time I was there it was in 1993 and I was several years younger (and several kilos lighter). Plus, life had not yet made me the person I am now.

Fifteen years ago I didn't care about where I stayed. A ramshackle series of cottages on the beach was good enough. I remember there was no air-conditioning, the bed was lumpy and the floor boards rickety. But none of us in the group paid the slightest attention to it while we stuffed our faces with food from the stalls on the beach, played frisbee and frolicked in the sea.

Fifteen years on, Anu prefers a comfortable room. Definitely one with an AC and a big soft bed. She eats at the restaurant and lazily strolls along the beaches, enjoying the sunset.

I was taken aback when I thought about how different things were now. But just as I was patting myself on the back for having become dignified and elegant, one of the waiters asked me if I would like to hire a motorbike and go see Spice Garden. I perked up at once. Discussions revealed that Spice Garden was spread across several acres and that they grew all kinds of spices there. It was about an hour away from where I was staying. The next day found me on a motorbike (which made some very interesting and faintly alarming noises) zooming down the roads of Goa. And I thought to myself, Ah, there's the pattern. Anu on a bike. Several wrong turns later, I reached Spice Garden.

Note to self: In order to see a new place you don't need to go somewhere new ... you just need to look at it through different eyes.

It is always lovely to see your country through the eyes of a foreigner. A couple from Spain and a man from Canada were part of the group that the guide was escorting around the estate. I watched them look keenly at arecanut trees, smell cloves and stare curiously at cardamoms.

That set me off on a different trip. I started looking at everything around me through the eyes of a non-Indian and I found several things that were so very quaint. Have you heard of a forex service called 'Hypnotic'? They also handle 'bike rentals'. Have you watched the sun set as you perched precariously on a railing in an abandoned park? Held a seashell in one hand and a bar of chocolate in another and wondered which one to drop? Walked unannounced into a church and kept walking down the corridors, expecting to be stopped but finding that no one bothered to do so?

Each experience made me wonder what we miss out on as we go about our busy lives. As I drove back, I smelt fuel. I smiled. I love the smell of petrol. What a gorgeous smell ... then it occurred to me that I am not supposed to be smelling petrol. This was taking enjoying experiences too far, surely. I stopped the bike and discovered a leak. I thought about starting it again but got worried about the possibility of the petrol tank exploding... Yes, I know I can be a bit melodramatic. Can't help it.

I pushed the bike to a roadside hotel and left it with the sweet Nepali boys who worked there, hopped on to a local bus and landed in Panaji minus the bike. Naturally, I was tired and hungry. I had been told that Ritz Classic was a fantastic place to eat at so I set off in search of the hotel, after calling for a replacement bike.

As I rode back to my hotel on the second bike, I smiled as I thought, some things never change. I might love a comfortable room and prefer strolling on the beach now, but I still love food, I love the feel of the wind on my face as I ride a bike, and I am still unfazed when things go wrong on one of these trips.

The other thing that I think is crucial to being happy is the ability to laugh at oneself. After all, if I hadn't been curious about Spice Garden I wouldn't have hired the bike in the first place. So when my curiosity lands me in situations that could have been avoided, being able to laugh at myself stands me in good stead.

Yes. I am a curious person by nature. If I were a cat I would have been on my nth set of nine lives. If you tell me I am not supposed to do something, I like to know why. I am not being rebellious, I just like to have good reason to follow someone else's advice. After all, why should I want to do that when I can get into spectacular trouble following my own?

Sometimes my overwhelming sense of curiosity makes me deaf to warnings and I merrily bumble forward and make a right ass of myself. And when that happens everyone, including me, has a good laugh. So now that you know how this story ends, let me tell you the story.

Graham and I were returning from a holiday in Rome. On reaching the airport, we found that there were four possible terminals and as luck would have it, the terminal we had to get to was the farthest. Already miffed that our holiday was over, Graham and I were none too happy about the long trek to the boarding gate but since we had no choice, we grumpily marched through the airport. We handle situations like these in different ways. While Graham is focused on reaching the end of this unwanted exercise session, I gawk at everything along the way, trying to absorb as much as I can.

We strode past shops and foreign exchange desks and the usual kiosks that seem to be scattered inside airports all over the world. My eyes swept past a stand with a touch screen on it. With no change in pace, I veered sharply towards it. It had lots of options on the screen and one said car park information. I've no idea why I did what I did but I reached forward and touched the info button. I heard a vague murmur in the background which I later realized was Graham saying, 'I don't think you should do that.'

As I touched the screen a pop-up announced, 'Call in progress.' I stared at it in dismay and looked around in panic for the disconnect button. Of course, I didn't find it.

'Do you really want to be doing this?' I heard Graham say this time. I turned to tell him I didn't know how to disconnect the call when, much to my chagrin, someone appeared on the screen. To add to my discomfort, it was a man in a rather official-looking uniform.

I was mortified but I stood my ground, despite being tempted to run. I said, 'Sorry, I was just looking for information.' Imagine my horror when the man at the other end signalled that he couldn't hear me and put on his headphones as he activated the camera above the screen. Now I could see my mug on the screen. I wondered if they would fine me or charge me for the video call. In my periphery, I could see Graham edging away so that he wasn't seen on camera, leaving me to sort out my own mess. My face began to burn.

'Sorry! It was a mistake,' I said into the screen quickly, hoping he would understand.

Instead he leaned forward and said, 'Si?'

My face turned redder, if that's possible. Now if there is one thing Italian men respond to it is a smile on the face of a woman. So I did the only thing I could. I smiled sweetly and waved and said, 'Thank you. Bye!' He lived up to my stereotype of the Italian male and grinned back at me and waved before disconnecting.

I hastily walked away from the machine towards Graham, who was standing nearby looking quite amused. The first thing he said was, 'Your face is red.'

Like I needed to hear that. 'Yeah, yeah. Let's go,' I said and resumed walking towards our original destination.

As he trailed behind me, Graham remarked, 'I'm going to tell Amma and Appa that you've been naughty.' I could hear the suppressed laughter in his voice.

I began to chuckle too. 'That was funny, wasn't it?' I said,

> **Note to self:**
> Expressing your
> ignorance is
> sometimes the only
> way to get rid of it.

turning around. 'I should tell them. They will find it hilarious.'

They always do when I make an ass of myself. But one thing I know – this wasn't the first time and it certainly won't be the last. But looking at the sunny side, if you will, at least now I know how those stand-alone touch screens work.

OLD-FASHIONED
MODERN ME

I am a curious combination of the conservative and the modern. As I bungle forth in life, I try to keep pace with technological advances even when my natural resistance to change holds me back.

Having studied in BITS Pilani and with two Master's degrees, I am not as unaccustomed to developments in technology as I appear. (The correct response to that is, 'You couldn't be!') Yet I tend to stay on the fringes of development. I have a BlackBerry and I resisted buying an iPad for the longest time. I was certain that the iPad was going to be popular but I wasn't going to run out and buy one just because someone was raving about it. In fact I wasn't sure the iPad (or iPhone) warranted all the fuss. I was convinced that my needs were met perfectly by my BlackBerry and clunky laptop.

But the nice thing about me (or so I would like to think) is that though I have convictions, if I am put in a situation where I have to change or question them, I am capable of doing that. So when my new corporate assignment meant I needed an iPad, I quickly went out and bought one. I still work on my heavy laptop but I am equally comfortable with the iPad.

While I am not fazed by hardware, my experience with the internet as a mode of communication and relationship building has left me with a whole new set of convictions. What a different world cyberspace is!

There is a forum for *Koffee* where people used to write in and I responded. You'd think there is a difference between being Anu and being the host of *Koffee with Anu*, but I was basically myself on that forum. The forum was a fairly useful tool as far as the programme was concerned and there were suggestions from viewers that we were able to implement. But when people assumed they could say anything they liked and expected me to quietly accept, I became scathing. Not a good reaction, I suppose. But why is it that one person is allowed to state his/her views and the other cannot simply because he/she is well-known? This is how I'm made and I responded regularly on the forum for more than three years. I was completely irreverent, unfazed by people threatening to go and watch some other programme unless I made certain changes, and always mindful of the fact that everything is transient and comes to an end. I accepted criticism that I thought was justified, shrugged off what I thought was not, defended that which needed to be defended and politely thanked those who sent in positive feedback. Requests to change my approach, attitude and costume were shot down with nary a qualm.

Then I discovered Orkut. What a different world that was. At first I was delighted when school friends and other people I knew started networking with me. It was wonderful to be in touch with people I had not spoken to in ages – until strangers started wanting to add me. I am fiercely protective of my private life. I am also extremely organized about compartmentalizing people and their place in my life. I have my school friends and classmates on Orkut. Very close friends are not on Orkut but in my phone book. And people I've met once or twice, well, they are simply out there. I put up a tag line that said '*Anu doesn't add strangers*' and I got add requests. My scrapbook warned them they would contract rabies – I got add requests. People who had met me in passing would write in saying, '*I am not a stranger.*' Of course there were also the '*Hello I want to make friendsheep with you*' and '*I think you are sexy, will you add me*' requests, which also I ignored. It began to get stressful until I unceremoniously started rejecting requests from anyone who did not fit my description of who I wanted on my Orkut list. I only wanted to network with people I wouldn't otherwise be in regular contact with. And this was turning out to be an intrusion. But once I gritted my teeth and decided not to worry about hurting people's feelings by rejecting their requests, things pretty much calmed down.

And do you remember Okcupid? Gosh, now THAT was fun! Okcupid was a site that popped up on an advertisement one day. I followed the link and it ended up being a dating site. It asks you multiple-choice questions and also asks you how your ideal partner would answer the same question. Then it makes some calculations and throws up a list of complete strangers who are compatible with you.

I was curious to see what kind of a person a software would say is compatible with me so I checked out some of the profiles. And I wondered how someone who communicated so badly (and I am not talking syntax and good English here – there were statements about what they expected from life and what they could give that completely scrambled my brain) could be 65 per cent compatible with me. Maybe they lied in their responses, in which case it simply meant that they could retain an image while they answered multiple-choice questions but when they described themselves in an open-ended format, they displayed certain traits that they otherwise camouflaged. I suppose you can fool some people some of the time but not all the people all the time.

I was on super analytical mode, wondering how the software worked and marvelling at the fact that thousands of questions are asked in a random order and each person's response tracked. And there were so many members! What a database it must need!

I got propositioned by several men and the smoothness with which the entire operation took place made me believe that it was something they were quite used to. What they didn't dare do in real life, they could do behind the protective shield of cyberspace. I was amused but it bored me after a while so I went back to Orkut and decided to see how anonymity defined interactions. Although I was using a pseudonym, my profile contained truth. As for what I did for a living, I wrote '*I shoot people and chat*' – an allusion to the role I play as a cop and to the talk show. Of course I had also mentioned that I work in film and television.

I thought it was fairly vague but some smart aleck deduced who I was. He had added me and I'd received a notification about it. Since I was in analytical mode, I wrote to him saying: '*You don't even know me... What are you doing adding me?*' Do you know what his response was? '*It is wonderful to see a lady like you here ...*' and so on, and in the end he wrote: '*This is what too much Koffee can do to you – if you get my drift.*'

I froze when I read that. Do you know how uneasy it makes you feel when you think you are in disguise and some stranger pricks your balloon of security? I didn't like it at all. I thought for a bit and responded, '*Well, you might want to watch out for too much coffee. Coffee is a diuretic, I am told.*' And then I quietly deleted my profile.

There are so many social networking sites out there. After much experimenting, I came to the conclusion that for someone like me, it could not be the starting point for any friendship. It could only be a tool that sustains communication. I was convinced that the internet was full of frustrated men who were there just because they wanted sex. I was certain that they were not there to build lasting relationships. While I wasn't sure if I myself was ready for a lasting relationship, I knew that a furtive affair with a stranger definitely wasn't what I wanted.

In the real world, the men in my life were either great friends or people who couldn't see past my celebrity status. While I have never contemplated a relationship with the former, I tire of the latter fairly quickly. And with everyone in the virtual world being a sex maniac, I had resigned myself to being single the rest of my life. Even when my brother met his future wife online, my reaction was a faintly cynical, 'Works for him, I suppose.'

Like I said, a whole new set of convictions ... or so I

thought, until Graham happened. I met Graham online and four years later I was married to him and living in London. How strange life is. And when I look back I realize that in some ways things worked out because we met online; Graham didn't know who I was when we started out. In fact, when we first met, he was startled that people wanted my autograph. He told me, 'If I had known you were famous, I would not have been comfortable approaching you at all.' As for me, I felt safe with him because he didn't want me for my celebrity status or what I can do or buy.

I am not going to pretend to know what makes a relationship work. I don't. But I do know this: sometimes you have to go out on a limb just to find out whether something works. It is always a risk but it's best to make it a calculated one.

> **Note to self:**
> Having convictions is good. But it is important to know which convictions need to be set aside and when.

My relationship with the internet as a platform of communication fluctuates between wonder and horror.

Milestones: I wonder why we have them. Is it to reassure ourselves that we are making progress? Or is it to tell others that we are not as useless as we appear to be? Whatever the reason, the place where this is most obvious is on Facebook status updates.

I look at updates that talk about everything from a child winning a race to a grandmother passing away and I watch as the lines between what should and shouldn't be shouted from rooftops blur. I remember one *Koffee* shoot where my guest mentioned that someone was surprised that she had not read their Facebook update. Which, by the way, mentioned that someone else had committed suicide. Huh? Excuse me? I wanted to ask her if she had lost touch with reality. But then I wondered if I was the one who had lost touch with progress.

Whatever the verdict is, (Confession #1: I must admit that it is convenient.) it is certainly easier to write that you miss someone than to go out and do something about it. Facebook in that sense is a great way to fool yourself. A few clicks, a couple of words tapped desultorily on your keyboard and you create the illusion of having 'connected' with someone. And if you are too lazy to do that, you can always click the 'Like' button.

I am not above fooling myself either. Except I make sure that at every opportunity I have face time with my friends. But I do get this warm fuzzy feeling when I see photographs taken twenty years ago and read the comments from the once-young people in those photographs. Including yours truly.

And have you noticed how sugary sweet everyone is on Facebook? Well, most people anyway. One only has to update with 'My darling baby turned twelve' and within seconds the congratulations come pouring in for the darling baby. Change your profile picture and regardless of how easily you could be mistaken for a monkey, the comments rave about how gorgeous you look and how 'you have not changed at all'.

While these kinds of updates are no great source of irritation, there are some that always get on my nerves. These are from those who wallow in misery. Their status

Note to self: Stay connected on Facebook but stay connected to reality as well.

updates tempt me to 'unfriend' them rightaway. I can't stand people who always moan about their lot in life. Worse still are those who are not honest enough to admit they are moaning and instead couch their moaning statements in false courage. For example, 'Back hurts like crazy, cracked head on door, all alone at home. But the gentle sound of the waves on the beach soothes me.' That kind of statement. Am I supposed to jump in and say, 'Ooh, how brave and how typical of you to notice nature's beauty amidst all that pain.'? (Confession #2: I have my share of drama queens in real life and the fact that I cannot do in real life what I can on Facebook – which is unfriend or ignore – has been a constant source of frustration to me.)

On the other hand, it has been wonderful to connect to my college mates. How else would I have known that one of my friends was on a TV show in America? That another's son was a child prodigy? Or that someone had developed a wicked sense of humour? And then there are the milestones – the years crossed, countries seen, friends met and jobs lost and won, the marriages and divorces... And once again I ask myself what motivates people to put up such updates. All we need to do is let our real world of contacts know what's going on in our lives.

I have joined the gaggle somewhat and do update my status once in a while but mainly to reflect on my lunch menu or the miles I have covered. I once walked 26 kilometres and proudly updated my status message. But then I added, 'Jalebis here I come,' which deflected all the well-meaning comments and instead brought in the teasing remarks that I so enjoy.

Not for me the shouting from the rooftops – probably because I have nothing to shout about. Life is good. I am happy, healthy and content. While that is something that is worth proclaiming to the whole world, I can't be bothered. Wait a minute – didn't I do exactly that now? Look at me all cleverly couching my trumpeting in careless disregard. Blame it on Facebook. But I meant to write about people and their motives. This was not supposed to be an analysis of the advantages and disadvantages of Facebook. Am I being boring and repeating what *The Social Network* has already spoken about? You will have to forgive me. I didn't see the movie. (Confession #3: I was too busy updating my status.)

Having said that, I have been told that I am one of the most networked people ever. I am not quite sure that's a compliment but I have noticed that I do tend to stay in touch with people I like. Even if they have been in my life for a short while, I remember to stay connected. And I use whatever platform I can to ensure this – Facebook, LinkedIn, BlackBerry, email or, more recently, Whatsapp. Living in London has underlined how important technology is in order to nurture friendships. How else would I stay in touch with all my friends who live so far away from me?

But then friendships are somewhat mysterious. Just as some plants survive with regular watering while others need plant food to survive and still others die despite having both,

Note to self: It's good to have a few low-maintenance plants in my garden of friends.

some of my friendships have flourished and some have died. I equate the interactions on technological platforms to regular watering and the physical time I spend with them to plant food.

PEOPLE

S mall things make a big difference.

Even if it is acknowledging someone as you walk past them. Appa always says, 'It doesn't cost anything to be nice to people.' As usual he is right. Two words can change a relationship and make things very different. No, I am not referring to 'get lost' – although they are two very useful words to have in your repertoire. I am talking about 'good morning'.

When I go down to the car park in the early hours of the morning, the watchman's son is usually there. Most people in my apartment just go about their work ignoring whoever is on duty but I find it difficult to do that unless I am really in a 'get lost' mood. So I usually say 'good morning'. When I moved into the apartment several years ago, the watchman was taken aback when I first said good morning to him. But soon he started enjoying saying it back and now he tries to beat me to it. It's the same with his son.

The maid who cleans the apartment corridors almost shouts out her good morning to me. She seems to get a thrill out of doing that. The watchman's son wishes me good morning as if he sincerely means it. The watchman

165

from the apartment opposite waves to me and says his good morning. As I get into the car, the newspaper delivery boy wishes me. I drive out and as I turn onto the road, I see the vegetable vendor pushing her cart. She smiles at me and waves. I wave back. If I had been walking, she would have said good morning too.

As I sit here now and think about the various accents, intonations and pronunciations in which those two words are delivered, the one thing that shines through is the cheerfulness. There is no subservience but almost a kind of glee. At first I thought it was the thrill of saying something in English that appealed to them. After all, except for the watchman's son, the rest probably hadn't even been to school. But it seemed to be about more than that. Then I thought that maybe it is because they think they are dealing with a 'celebrity'. But I got the same response even before I started working in films and television.

It is the contact. Not contact with someone deigning to greet a lesser creature but with a person who treats them like a fellow human being instead of part of the scenery.

How many times have we walked past the watchman and not paid any attention to him? And even if he wished us, how many of us merely nod in acknowledgement as if to say that he is inferior and therefore we *expect* him to wish us? How many times have we dealt with someone and gone directly to what we wanted instead of taking a few seconds to acknowledge him or her as a person? I don't know about you but I have done these things many times. I still do.

But when I catch myself doing it (and if I am not in a 'get lost' mood) I take time out, just a few seconds, to acknowledge that person, and I can see that it makes the moments a little more pleasant. I have tried this on parking attendants, waiters in restaurants, mechanics, flower sellers, fishermen, garbage collectors. It startles them at first but they enjoy it. They might think I am mad but they smile. They seem happy – so how does it matter?

It's not as if I jump on everyone I come across to say good morning – now *that* would be odd. I am talking about the spirit behind the whole thing. However, I am by nature a chatty person. So by saying good morning if I trigger off a conversation, I don't mind. I recall travelling with someone once who was appalled that I was chatting with the man driving our car. She seemed to think it was a waste of time. Ah, the old 'it is beneath your dignity to interact with a certain class of people' thing. It's a pity so many people hide behind this bias. Sure, there are ruffians and hooligans who are best left alone but to tar everyone with the same brush seems to me a waste of one's life. After all, if the 'good morning' leads to a situation that you don't want to be in, you can always use the other two words.

For me, this approach works. It is almost as if I feed off the happiness that these small gestures generate. Soppy? Perhaps. But it is lovely to start the day the way I do and even nicer to extend it to some – if not all – of my interactions during the day.

This is probably why people often remark about what a happy chipmunk I am and I am often asked how that

> **Note to self:** Do not forget the impact that small courtesies have on other people. And how much it adds to making the day that much more pleasant, for them as well as for you.

is so. For a long time I didn't give it much thought. But one day I decided to sit down and think about it. Why is it that I am perceived to be 'always happy' and 'always energetic'? It's not as if I've had a completely blessed life. I have had my fair share of slaps in the face and pats on the back from a life that has often been more capricious than is normal. So what is it that helps build this particular happy energetic image? I couldn't pinpoint it but I think it has something to do with the fact that I find myself very amusing.

Even as far back as my school days, I remember that if I tripped and fell down, the first thought that entered my head was how funny and ridiculous I must look and I ended up laughing at myself. This attitude followed me to college and has stayed with me through my adult life. I find myself amused by my own fears and worries. Don't get me wrong – when I am worried and fearful, I am convinced that my world is about to collapse into shambles around me within the next few minutes. But as the minutes pass and the world continues to remain the way it always has been, I sheepishly realize that I have panicked and then the sheepishness gives way to a smile and the smile sometimes explodes into laughter.

While this is the reaction I have to the manageable fears, the unmanageable ones are accorded far more respect. They get relegated to the back of my mind, swept under the proverbial carpet. Very sensible. Naturally the ones that stubbornly refuse to get swept under have to be faced. It's quite a nuisance, considering this time would be better spent eating carrot cake and drinking coffee.

When it is not panic it is suspicion. Is it just me or do

you feel a sense of distrust when it comes to computer-generated bills?

I am very suspicious of my service provider's bill when it comes to my cell phone. I get this feeling that they are sneakily billing me in excess. If only I could catch them at it...

Every month when my cell-phone bill arrives, I stare at it for the longest time and then go through the numbers on my call list. Earlier, I was not averse to thinking that people had nothing better to do than to grab my cell phone and make calls on it without my knowledge. This assumption died a natural death when I realized that everyone including my vegetable vendor has a cell phone they can happily afford. So now my gimlet eyes focus only on my itemized bill.

The other day I collected my bill from my dad's office like I do every month. It was longer than usual and I thought this was because I had checked my mail on the phone a few times. When I looked at the amount it was a thousand rupees more than what I usually run up. I sat up straight. Finally an opportunity to prove that these guys were cheating me!

I flipped over to the STD calls list and almost crowed in delight when I found several calls made to an unknown number. I recognized some of the other numbers but not this one. The calls were spaced minutes apart. Obviously the cell-phone company had decided to cheat me of three-hundred-odd rupees. It isn't a huge amount – but with three hundred rupees from one subscriber and a huge customer base, we are talking several crores. Even as I was raring to call them and tell them I had caught them out on their dirty trick, I wondered – what if someone had grabbed my phone and made calls? So I called up the number to check who it was. A lady answered and I explained why I was calling. She said she had been to Madras on the dates I had mentioned but that she doesn't know me. She sounded too polished to be a friend of my maid or my assistant. I apologized for disturbing her and then, brimming with self-righteousness, I called the service provider.

In a strident tone I said, 'I have a cell-phone number with your company. I have received my bill and it has several wrong billings.'

The extra-polite voice at the other end was unfazed. (You know how those voices can get with their attitude of: 'Oh look, here is an irate customer – if I speak to her in a singsong manner, she will cool down.') 'Can I put you on hold, madam?'

For a moment I wondered how he would react if I said, 'No, I demand justice this very instant!' But that was a little too melodramatic even for me. So I put on my most growly voice and said, 'No problem, I will wait.' Implying that he would have to face the music when he returned.

He came back on the line after making *me* listen to some ghastly music for about a minute and said, 'Tell me, Ms Hasan.'

I repeated that there were wrong entries in my bill.

He said, 'Your bill dated 15 September 2008, madam?'

'My latest one!' I said impatiently and scanned the top of my bill for the date. 'The one dated 3 September 2008.' Gosh, couldn't they even get my billing date right? I rolled my eyes and started to say something else in a severe tone. My eyes continued scrolling down the bill details on the first page and I froze ... and almost burst out laughing. This was my Uncle's bill. The numbers I recognized were all numbers that belonged to family and friends. And that had let me to assume that it was my bill.

Instead of the scathing comment I had intended to make, I was forced to say, 'Sorry. This is not my bill. I assumed it was.' And before he could laugh at me, I said thank you and ended the call. For a good few minutes after, I sat with a stupid grin on my face, imagining what an idiot he must have thought I was.

You know what they say – 'When you assume you make an ASS of U and ME.' And considering the number of situations I get into because of my assumptions, I must love making an ass of myself.

While one part of my nature is to make assumptions, the other part is the complete opposite – the one that is unashamed to say 'I don't know'.

Once I was invited to a book launch in London. Although I have been to a handful, I am almost always unsure of what one is supposed to do at these events. Patrick French had been researching for his book and

> **Note to self:**
> Suspicion is a healthy thing, keep it alive – until it makes you look like an idiot. That's when you need to rein it in with practicality, but don't kill it completely.

you know how eager I am to shoot off my mouth about our country and what I believe our people are like. Since he had miraculously managed to distil some sense from my usual gibberish and actually quote me in his book, I was kind of keen on attending the launch.

It was in a part of London that I was not familiar with

(which covers about ninety per cent of London). After changing two tubes and walking about with a befuddled look on my face, it occurred to me that I was slightly lost. Unashamed as always of displaying my ignorance, I asked a school girl where Marylebone Street was. She pointed to a board ten feet away which had Marylebone Street written on it in large letters. Well, you can't say you are unashamed to display your ignorance and then look bashful when it happens. So I smiled and thanked her and set off down the street.

I am proud to say that I arrived at exactly the time specified on the invite. Patrick looked quite lost himself when he saw me. But he beamed when I walked up to say hello and led me across to his uncle, who started talking about his Grenadier days. I love listening to old people reminisce about the past and this was no exception. Slowly, people started milling about and someone else started talking to uncle and I was left staring vacantly at a crowded room. I noted another Indian lady doing the same and I thought I would go and check if she was Patrick's wife.

Turned out she was the high commissioner's wife. Oops. But I was unfazed and we struck up a conversation. Soon she was telling me about the book she was writing. Invariably the conversation turned to books – Patrick's in particular – and my usual ability to be unashamed about my ignorance started to wane.

Around me were some of the most well-read people I've ever met – Patrick, a man who had authored Naipaul's biography among other very successful books, the high commissioner's wife, who had penned a few books and was extremely well-read, the gentleman who was in the Grenadiers who had authored several books and made references to several more. And among all these people was poor old Anu trying valiantly not to show how completely out of depth she was.

There is one thing that always comes to my rescue when I am in such situations, and that is my ability to listen and to keep the conversation going. I had never needed that ability more. And so the evening went on, with people referring to books I had no idea about and me sidestepping neatly to ask them something else about that very book without directly saying I hadn't read it or implying that I had. It was quite fun, really.

I did not make the usual mistake that people do in these situations – which is to try and draw the conversation towards a topic I *did* know about. Which was, to be honest, everything and nothing. A little knowledge is a dangerous thing, and I am a loose cannon when it comes to it. I just continued talking and leading the conversation on. We finally came to a point where one of them turned and asked me something along the lines of 'Have you read *Tibet, Tibet?*' Without pausing a beat, I replied, 'No. Did you like it?' That set off another discussion. And at that very instant I realized something.

It did not matter whether I knew something. It did not matter that I had not read the books they were referring to. They wanted someone to listen and they had found that in me. That was all they cared about.

This is how it works in most social situations. You don't have to be a know-it-all to be popular. Even if you are ignorant you can be the soul of the party as long as you are willing to be educated. Of course you also have to put up with the occasional bore who drones on and on about saving butterflies or cataloguing tapeworms, but that is a small price to pay. Plus you walk away knowing that much more than you did when you walked in. (Even if it is about tapeworms.)

The evening drew to a close, Patrick made his speech, we clapped, and another half hour later it was time to leave. I had made a new friend in the high commissioner's wife and another one in the Grenadier's wife.

> **Note to self:** If you are uncomfortable in a situation – listen. It will always give you a clue on what to say next.

Although I must confess I still haven't read *Tibet, Tibet*. Yet another occasion to display my ignorance looms ahead.

DIVORCE

I would be the first person to admit that my life is not just full of funny moments and meaningful highlights. It's just that I choose to remember those moments that have defined me as a person. I have had my fair share of bad times, depression, crying sessions. But as amma says, I am like a Thanjavur bommai – a bobbing doll. You can knock it down but because of the way it is designed, it will always bob right back up. And while with every blow I change a little, I cling to my ability to get back on my feet. Life is like boxing – you don't lose when you fall down; you lose when you fail to get up.

And so it has been with me. I have fallen down many times. And it has hurt. But after wallowing in self-pity for a while, I pick myself up, dust myself and carry on.

After one of the biggest debacles in my life, a friend commented, 'You are such a little warrior' and that image got stuck in my mind. I am a warrior. A little one, but nevertheless a fighter.

I think one of the saddest periods in my life was when I was going through my divorce. After ten years I had decided that the marriage was not for me. I had stayed for many reasons and realized that none of them was right. So there I was, walking out of a marriage with no money and no prospects. I wasn't even leaving him for another man. I was leaving him for myself.

Even now, as I sit down to write about that time, it gives me an uneasy feeling in the pit of my stomach. I remember the tears, the fear and the unshakeable sense of having been a failure. But I also remember the incredible support my parents extended me. My father's response after the initial shock was, 'You needn't have waited ten years,' and my mother's, 'Your happiness is what matters. Come away if you are not happy.'

Neither of them pointed out that I had chosen to marry him knowing they were not completely convinced it was the right choice. There's parental wisdom for you. Which is also why I will never become a parent. I don't have the patience nor the wisdom for it.

If my parents were supportive, the rest of the family didn't interfere either. They asked me if I was sure and that was that. Neither the Hasan family nor my mother's side of the family said, 'Oh no! You should try and make it work.' I suppose ten years was enough time for a woman of reasonable intelligence to figure out whether it could or couldn't work.

I spent many a day wondering what was wrong with me. You see, my ex was not a cruel man. He didn't beat me, he didn't have an affair (at least not that I know of) and he didn't insult me or abuse me emotionally. So what was the problem? Ambition. I didn't have enough. Money was important to me but living life within a framework of rules mattered more.

So I was torn between his ambition and ability to bend and sometimes break rules and my natural middle-class fear of breaking the law. I do understand that in order to succeed in business some corners need to be cut. And I am sure that if I wanted something badly enough I would happily cut not just the corner but a fair portion of the side as well. I just didn't want it badly enough. I didn't need a Gucci bag to feel successful. I didn't need to take my friends to posh places to feel important.

I didn't have the ability or the maturity to separate my equation with him as a person from my equation with him as a colleague. It was one of the toughest things for me because I had set up the company and

> **Note to self:**
> Morality is usually not just lack of opportunity but also often lack of desire.

he retired from the army in order to take over.

With each day I sank lower and lower, doing everything half-heartedly. I even agreed to do the line production for the movie *Mumbai Xpress* just so that he could get a foothold into film production. That was the last straw, and it made me see clearly where I was headed.

While I am good at administration and logistics, I did not enjoy being a line producer. I lost my temper, cried and was afraid all the time. In the end I was left with a sense of desolation. I am not the kind of person who can set aside my personal dislikes to be a foil for someone else and let him pursue his dreams – not when I seem to be an integral means of achieving it. Nobility is not a particular strength of mine.

And then something else happened that shocked me into clarity. The movie had been released and it was time for me to go back to Calcutta and I was miserable that I had to leave. I knew what I was going back to. I asked myself, 'When will this end?' And a voice within responded, 'Either I have to die or he has to.' The severity of that jolted me.

Yes, I was sane enough to know that it was an illogical response triggered by my usual melodrama. I also knew that as I slid into depression it might start to make sense. I did not stop to think any further about what that sentence meant. The decision I couldn't make in ten years I made in ten minutes. It was time to leave.

> **Note to self:** Do not give up easily. But it is important to identify the point when hanging onto something is more destructive than letting go.

No amount of emotional blackmail would sway me. If it was a choice between my survival and his, I had to choose mine.

I do not mean to trivialize my decision or underplay the pain and loneliness. I think I have rehashed the past sufficiently in order to share with you the lesson I learnt.

My life changed for the better after the divorce. My mother says I blossomed. A little late for me to 'blossom' but I think I understand what she meant. I broke free of another's expectations and started building my own. I was in many ways a sadder person yet in many others a happier one.

I did not come out of the divorce disillusioned or bitter. I owe this to my parents and to three of my friends – Kripa, Ranga and Abe. I still remember how Kripa stood by me during my lowest time. This was before I had made up my mind to go ahead with the divorce and I was consumed by a general feeling of hopelessness and of being trapped. She was the only one who knew things in my marriage were not quite as brilliant as I painted them to be. But Kripa is the kind of person who can just be there, letting you know you have her support without forcing you into a heart-to-heart. And that was such a comfort at the time.

I wasn't clear in my head about where I wanted to go – I was making mistakes as I struggled to cope with my failing marriage and I was compounding my mistakes by lying that I was happy and that everything was hunky dory. That we were a team and I wanted what he wanted. Kripa would come to meet me after work. At that time I was living out of a hotel room in Mumbai while *Mumbai Xpress* was being produced. We would sit quietly, one of us reading a Mills and Boon, the other watching TV. Then one of us would say, 'Dinner?' and we would order room service, eat and go to sleep. In the morning she went off to work. So did I. This was a pattern that continued for most of the time that I was in Mumbai.

My faith in men, on the other hand, was upheld by two of the very best – Ranga and Abe. While from Kripa I got complete support, from these two I got practical sound advice.

> **Note to self:** Non-verbal support is sometimes the most comforting of all.

When I was going through a particularly painful part of the divorce negotiations, they both cautioned me against getting angry. I remember Abe telling me, 'His reaction stems from pain. Don't let that force you to behave badly.'

I feel a residual sadness as I write about that phase in my life. But the lessons I learnt were priceless. Like my father said, I need not have waited ten years to make my decision.

But I did. I didn't have the courage to go through with the divorce until I was absolutely sure. So no regrets there.

After the divorce I became more honest, I was open and accepting of my faults. I've noticed that I make people uncomfortable with my (sometimes abrasive) honesty. It's not worth hiding your discomfort or your motives. I've learnt that being polite when you don't need to, overly considerate of other people's feelings when you shouldn't be, and not vocalizing your limitations only lead to misery.

Note to self: Life is not meant to be a sacrifice. One's personal happiness cannot be at the cost of another's.

Oddly enough, I did not have to face the stigma of being a divorcee – or perhaps it was I who refused to allow others to treat me differently. I was open about the fact that I was divorced and a warning glance usually dissuaded curious questions. But I didn't realize how much of a battle it can be for other women until I faced a group of chauvinists in one of my shows.

If I love *Koffee with Anu* for giving me the opportunity to meet and learn from achievers and successful professionals, I love *Kannaadi* for the perspective it gave me on the lives of others. I was shooting for *Kannaadi* and the topic was divorce. Being a divorcee myself, I had no bias against divorce. This doesn't mean I was unaware that women can be unscrupulous. I have read about cases where the man is the wronged one. So I was expecting a fair representation from the men's side and a strong one from the women.

Imagine my surprise when I went onto the sets and found that the only divorced woman on the sets was me. There were married women and divorced men and single men, there were lawyers and activists – but not a single divorced woman amongst the participants.

I was quite curious to see how the discussion would proceed. It started off sedately enough. One of the older women pointed out that with the dilution of the joint family, husband and wife had no buffers. As a result, arguments that could have been diffused by the presence as well as the involvement of elders got blown out of proportion, causing irreparable damage to the relationship. She concluded by saying that while a joint family may not be practical these days, one must strike a balance and families should spend more time together.

I could see her logic.

Another man pointed out that since most women work these days, husband and wife hardly got time after work to spend time together and understand each other. As a result relationships wear away. He concluded by saying that we need to strike a balance between our personal and professional lives.

I could see his logic too.

Then another man spoke up. 'All women are greedy and only care about money. They get divorced just so they can lay their hands on easy money!' I was taken aback by his vehemence and before I could react, a group of men applauded loudly. With each misogynistic statement of his, the applause grew louder.

I looked at the women in the forum and while some did make weak attempts to contribute to the discussion, not a single woman stood up to challenge the man's statement.

He went on to say that women are not brought up properly these days and they aren't willing to adjust.

As an anchor, it's not my place to get involved in the discussion. I am meant to steer it, not participate. But I couldn't help asking him if he thought that only women should adjust. He replied, 'I adjust too. I go buy vegetables for my wife.' My jaw dropped. Did he think he was actually being adjusting and accommodating just because he was buying vegetables? And what did he mean 'buy for his wife'? Didn't he eat the meals she cooked?

Another man jumped in and told us how his ex-wife wouldn't give him visitation rights. He was crying. He said he missed his son and that his enemy was another woman – namely, his mother-in-law. The men clapped again. I saw red.

I told them in a scathing tone: 'A man just shared his pain. What are you clapping about? What is there for you to rejoice about?' An uneasy silence fell over the entire set. But I wasn't done. I glared at the main misogynist and asked him, 'Are you married?'

He timidly replied, 'Yes.'

I wanted to ask him if his wife would also turn out to be the kind of person he thought all women were. But before I could (unwisely) put my thoughts into words, support came from an unlikely source.

It was from one of our panellists – a man. He said, 'There might be women who take advantage of the system and behave in an unscrupulous manner but not all women are like that. There have been enough cases where women have been treated so badly that divorce is the only solution for them if they wanted to survive.' I could hear rumbles of discontent from the other men. And then he added, 'The option of divorce is a blow to male chauvinism. Accept that.'

Even I wasn't expecting such a strong statement.

I am not quite sure I agree with him but I was curious to see the reaction of the group of men whom I was actually beginning to dislike. I wasn't disappointed. There was immediate outrage. Each one fought to shout over the other in his attempt to prove to the world that all women were evil. I watched them for a bit, allowing them to make asses of themselves on camera. It was the least I could do for my fellow women. When I had had enough of the noise, I stepped up and cut them short by putting my fingers in my mouth and whistling loudly (my dad taught me how to and I can deliver an eardrum-splitting whistle) It worked … they froze in surprise. I neatly stepped into the silence and finished the episode by saying that sometimes divorce is indeed an option but we should remember that it's the last one.

As finishing lines go, I quite liked it. I should have felt pleased. But as I walked away from the shoot that day it was with a sense of unease. I hadn't known that men like the ones I had just encountered existed in such large numbers. But misogynists are a fact of life – as are women who think all men are bastards. So accept it I must. What I couldn't digest was the fact that not one of the women stood up to defend their own kind.

How could they sit and watch while those men tarred every single woman with the same brush? Was it because they believed it? Was it because they were afraid to speak

Question to self:

In all important things in life, when taking a stance, a balance has to be struck ... but at what price? Do we keep quiet so we do not rock the boat? Or do we risk drowning in the displeasure of a male-dominated society?

out? Or was it because they didn't care?

Earlier, whenever I saw a wedding card, the images that came to mind were of lush Kanjeevaram saris, sparkling diamonds and glittering gold jewellery. But everyone knows that's not all that a wedding is about. I should know, considering I have seen my fair share of them. Regardless of divorce rates – or maybe because of them – marriage is a big step. And for me it was a decision I was reluctant to take a second time because of my divorce.

When I told my mother that Graham had proposed to me, she responded, 'So what's the problem? You say you are happy with him.' I was taken aback. This from a sixty-eight-year-old supposedly traditional lady who had never even laid eyes on a photograph of my British boyfriend?

I looked at her bemusedly and said, 'Amma, I don't even know if it will work out. I have made a mistake before. I don't want to make a mistake again.'

Her response was infinitely wise. 'If you are going to wait and see if it is going to work out, you will wait your entire life. Make up your mind that you want to make it work. And take the step.'

Amazing words that don't fail to move me even today. For they show not only her wisdom but also a mother's wish to see her daughter happy. That was the last little nudge that I needed to take the plunge.

The first year that Graham's parents visited us, Graham's mum called me aside to talk to me. I must admit to feeling a slight dread as I went and sat beside her. I couldn't help thinking I was going to be subjected to typical mother-in-law talk. She was going to tell me how I should take care of her beloved son.

I couldn't have been more wrong. There were many things that we spoke about but three things she said to me stood out:

Don't lose touch with your friends. Your friends are important and Graham has to understand that. As you grow older you will cherish the friendships very much. Take my word for it.

Don't ever give up work just because you are married. Your work defines a large part of who you are and will give you a lot of happiness.

Your money has to be deposited in your account, not in Graham's. I have seen many women do that. That is not how it is supposed to work.

I hadn't expected to hear this kind of advice from my mother-in-law, of all people. How amazingly practical and impartial. When I told Graham about her advice, he shrugged his shoulders and said, 'So? That's how it's supposed to be.' To him it was nothing unusual. This was one occasion where our cultural differences were working brilliantly in my favour. Who was I to complain? I didn't elaborate but vehemently agreed with him.

To anyone starting this wonderfully new journey I have this to say: there will be gloriously happy moments – cherish them. But it is not going to be all joy and laughter.

Note to self: You may not always want advice but by being receptive to those who are wiser, you will find something to steady you when you falter.

There will be difficult moments, ones that make you cry and feel desolate. During these times, the words of advice given to me by my mother and Graham's mother have served me well. Feel free to borrow them as and when the need arises.

ANGER, IMPATIENCE
AND ME

Anger and impatience are two emotions I have always struggled to control. Each time I get better at it, I congratulate myself. Each time I lose, I beat myself up and promise to handle the situation better the next time. But it isn't always that the control comes from within.

A friend and I had decided to start a fruit juice and smoothies chain. The aim was to create a profitable venture that would provide employment for women from the lower socio-economic strata. I had an administrative assistant who had this ability to make me laugh at the most unexpected moments. When everyone expected me to explode in fury, I ended up laughing because of her.

We were moving locations and I was very stressed with shifting equipment. They had forgotten to shift one of the pieces and I was furious. It was not a small machine and now we were going to have to organize a vehicle just to move a single piece of equipment.

I called the office and said, 'Belinda, can you please keep the machine ready near the steps? As soon as the lorry comes in, you can load it.'

She replied, 'Which steps, ma'am?'

Already at the end of my tether, I said in irritation, '*How many steps are there in the office, Belinda?*'

She replied patiently, '1, 2, 3 ... total twelve steps, ma'am.'

If I had not known for a fact that she was not being arrogant I would have fired her on the spot. But her statement had only one result – I burst out laughing.

There was a similar incident another time. The key to the drawer where we keep the cash and our sales deposit slips is hidden inside a cardboard box. Not that there is a huge amount of money in there – probably less than thousand rupees at any given time. My accountant came in to my room and asked for the deposit slips. I called Belinda and asked her to pull the key out of the drawer and give it to him. She nodded sagely, walked behind me, picked up the cardboard box and left the room. I looked up to see her walking out hugging the cardboard box, looking extremely serious, and I smiled. When she returned with the key and opened the drawer, I smiled at her and said, 'Good thinking, Belinda,' and she had this oh-so-proud look on her face which said, 'See what a genius I am? I didn't let on where the key was.' The smirk was too much and I couldn't help laughing.

Belinda had actually come to me looking for a maid's job. For some reason I felt she might be good at admin work and decided to train her. I never regretted it despite the fact that she was a little slow. She had a good heart and she really tried. She had the patience that more, supposedly intelligent, people did not. And most importantly, she

Note to self: Be open to triggers that might lighten a tense situation. There are more of them around than you think.

made me laugh at the most unexpected moments. I could have found a more qualified person for the job, but a more reliable one? I doubt it.

I still recollect the day Belinda came to tell me she wanted to resign. I was standing at the training table as she walked up to me. Her eyes were bloodshot and she looked as if she had been crying for a while. I was used to working with hysterical females, and being one myself, I knew the best thing to do was to pretend not to notice and continue working. But Belinda would have none of it. She insisted on going to my cabin with me, where she made me sit down and listen to her.

What she told me made me sigh at the familiar story – a drunkard for a husband, loans to contend with and two children to educate. At the end of it, she said, 'That's why, ma'am, I want to resign.'

I didn't get it. I asked her why.

Her response: 'I want to stay at home and take care of my husband.'

I looked at her and tried to figure out her logic. But she seemed determined, so I let her go. I often wonder how she is and what she is doing, whether her husband is still alive, whether her story was true. Someone told me that she had been stealing from the office all along. I later found that same person guilty of fraud.

I don't know why her brand

> **Note to self:**
> Sometimes trustworthiness is a phase. People go from one to the other. The trick is to trust them when they deserve it and protect your interests when they don't.

of incompetence made me laugh. What was it that she brought with her when she came into my life? I think it was tolerance.

It's a pity she left.

But anger and me, we have a constant battle. There was a phase when I thought that, as I grew older, instead of becoming more tolerant and patient, I was becoming more impatient and snappy. I am conscious of the fact that I can be very incisive in my choice of words, therefore I have to be extra careful when I get angry.

Every time I lose my temper, I feel as though I have lost a battle. Then again, each time I fight for control for a little bit longer than before. So there is some consolation.

I had just got off the phone with the secretary of a club. (I hung up on him, actually.) We started out on the wrong foot. His opening line was, 'Madam, you received an award from us a few years ago, do you remember? Now there is a function for someone else, so you have to come.' I bristled at the implication that I was indebted to them in some way but told myself he probably didn't know how to talk and politely replied that if I did not have shoot, I would certainly come. He brushed aside my acceptance and jumped in to say, 'Okay, by the way, I have seen many of your shows – that coffee ... that one ... I have a suggestion.'

I knew exactly where he was going. I had been doing the show for three years and for two of those years I had heard the refrain that I should choose guests from outside the film industry as well. The mistake I made was in pre-empting him by replying, 'Well, I am afraid you will have to speak to the channel, sir, because they are the final authority on guest selection.'

He replied, 'But I am a person who appreciates the show, you should listen to me and take my suggestion.'

Now I am normally well-behaved. I gritted my teeth, clamped down on my rising irritation and asked him to please go ahead. He said exactly what I knew he was going to say. I waited impatiently for him to finish his sentence before I replied, 'That's what I said, sir. Such suggestions have to be given to the channel, because they are the ones who decide.' (Now there was an edge of annoyance to my supposedly polite tone.)

If he had said 'Okay' and dropped the matter, I would have won. But he didn't. Instead, he said, 'YOU go tell them. I am not going to canvas for this.'

Kaboom!!! There went my self-control. The word 'canvas' tipped me over.

I said in a dangerously cold voice, 'If I speak politely does it in some way prevent you from understanding what I'm saying? Would you understand better if I got angry? Did I mention the word "canvas"? You chose to use the word.'

The man was obviously determined to make me lose. He countered in an aggressive tone, 'I am a viewer and you should listen to me.'

I had no option but to concede defeat. Which I did – and then let loose.

'I did not ask you to "canvas" for my show. I told you that your suggestions need to be directed to the channel. I did not ask you to call me. I find the way you speak offensive.

And if you think I am going to be quiet and listen to you, you are very mistaken. And I am NOT coming for your function!' On that note, I furiously disconnected the phone. (Although I suspect he did the same thing simultaneously after trying ineffectually to interrupt my tirade with 'Okay, I withdraw' or some such statement.)

The second I disconnected the phone, a sense of failure swamped me. I did not regret a single sentence that I had uttered. But I regretted getting angry and letting him see that I was.

The same thing happens during shoots. I hold onto my temper but when I am tired and when I am pushed, I snap. And then I feel I have failed. But I do confess that when I allow the fury to gain control, there is a malicious side of me that enjoys the cutting remarks, the incisive choice of words, the cleverness of my attack. I never use profanities nor do I insult. I always attack from a very safe position and it leaves the person frustrated that they cannot find a loophole to attack me in return. I ride the wave of anger, enjoy the crest and then come crashing down to the unforgiving sand of rational thoughts.

Sometimes I tell myself that I am no angel. So it is okay to get angry. When I calm down, if I have been in the wrong, I have no qualms about going up to the person concerned and saying, 'Sorry, I lost my temper.' But when I am not in the wrong, my ego refuses to allow me to do that. Humble pie was never my favourite dish.

So the battle continues. I have a shoot in a few days. This time I am prepared. There is one man who irritates the you-know-what outta me. The first day I shouted at him.

On the second day I snapped quietly. I am hoping that this time, even if I lose the occasional skirmish, I will win the battle. More importantly, I am hoping the third time is going to be lucky. For him.

While I struggle to control my temper, sometimes I feel fate conspiring against me, maliciously manipulating other people to keep testing me.

> **Note to self:**
> Changing an aspect of your personality is not impossible. The most important thing in life is to give up what you are for what you can become.

My friends tease me about my work–life balance. 'You take a flight to London like one would take the bus to Guduvanchery,' they say. A slight exaggeration but you get the point. The fact is that I travel often enough to be familiar with which seats to book, which security lane to follow in Dubai as I transit and which buffet counter to go to in the lounge in order to avoid the crowd.

I usually like to book a window seat as I am still childish enough to enjoy looking out of the window as we fly above deserts and across mountains and over clouds. I enjoy looking at the higgledy-piggledy fields as I land in London as much as I enjoy the sweeping expanse of the coast and the clumps of coconut trees as I land in Madras. You never grow out of some things.

This trip I had booked myself on the window seat as usual and when boarding was announced, I sauntered across to my seat and sat down, going through my usual ritual of taking out my moisturizer, lip balm and book. A young chap came in and settled next to me. As he frantically searched for his seatbelt, the experienced traveller that is me pointed out that he was sitting on it. I should know since I have done it often enough and I told him as much. He grinned at me in relief and after a few desultory attempts at conversation, each of us went back to what we were doing – me to my book and him to his texting. A lady came along, paused and then sat down in the aisle seat after exchanging a brief smile with me when I looked up. And so the three of us settled in peacefully.

Until I heard a voice. 'Excuse me, that's my seat. 26H.'

All three of us looked up to find this man standing in the aisle, looking at me.

'Oh?' I said and pulled out my boarding pass to check. It said 26K, which was the seat I was on. I told him as much.

'No. 26H is the window seat and you are on the wrong seat.'

I gently tried to point out the marking on the cabin hold, showing him how the picture of the window was next to the letter K. He would have none of it.

While this was happening, the lady in the aisle gently piped up, 'Oh, I have 26K as well. I thought you were sitting in my seat by mistake.' Great! Now two people thought I was in the wrong seat.

I looked at the man standing in the aisle and said, 'Maybe we need to call the stewardess to sort this out.'

His response to that took all of us by surprise. 'You both are the ones with the problem. My ticket is okay. You get up. And you call the stewardess.'

I stared at him in disbelief while he continued in a louder voice, 'That is MY seat. I want MY seat.'

I started grinning at this grown man behaving like a

child. Struggling to control the laughter that threatened to surface, I told him, 'Yours is actually the aisle seat. The problem is that this lady and I seem to have the same seat numbers for this window seat.'

No sooner had I uttered the last syllable than he pounced on me with, 'So you get up from my seat and call the stewardess and sort out the problem.'

I chuckled and said, 'How gallant you are to make two women get up so you can sit in the wrong seat!'

I could see he was about to have an apoplectic fit. So I excused myself, made the young chap move and stood in the aisle. The childish boor hastily slipped in to sit in the window seat. The lady and I smiled ruefully at each other.

'Quite rude, wasn't he?' she said.

I nodded. 'I think he was worried we would make him sit on the wings of the plane and flap his arms to get to Dubai.'

The young chap snorted as he tried to smother his laughter. Then he meekly asked if either of us would like his seat, adding that he didn't want to seem ungallant. I told him not to worry and we waited for the stewardess to come along. All along I knew that if two of us had the same seat, it only meant that one of us had been upgraded. And since my Guduvanchery-like travel put me on gold member status, in all likelihood it was me.

I remembered how I used to feel guilty about business class upgrades – this was before I became a frequent traveller. But this time I wasn't going to be noble. So when the stewardess came and told me I had been upgraded to business class on account of being a frequent flier, I consoled myself that I had in some way earned it. The satisfaction at

> **Note to self:** There are some things that you never grow out of and the pleasure you get out of them might trigger your sense of humour enough to help you stave off anger.

leaving Mr Boor behind outweighed any guilt I might have felt.

The lady smiled and said, 'So you got lucky.'

I replied, 'Looks like it. You have a good flight,' including the young chap in my parting line. Studiously ignoring Mr Boor, I triumphantly took my bag and book and sundry items and marched off to business class. It was only after I settled into my new seat that it occurred to me that I could have rubbed Mr Boor's face in it by making the stewardess tell him he was in the wrong seat. Dammit! My petty mind missed out on that childish pleasure!

As recently as a few weeks ago, I was thrown into the very same situation I had been in before. It was past 1 a.m. and we had been filming since 11 a.m. the previous day. I was tired and sleepy and hungry. Everyone else had finished their work and the only thing left for me was to record the parts where I, as the presenter, welcome back the viewers, announce the breaks, etc.

I requested that the floor become silent; it went unheeded. Everywhere people were chatting. Where I had once yelled for floor silence and launched into a tirade I now held back and tried my best to ignore the noise. But when someone walked right behind the camera with a huge white board, I lost my concentration and fumbled to a stop. Cut!

The next time, I had almost finished the line but someone

laughed loudly and I turned involuntarily in the direction of the sound. Cut!

I believe in floor silence when the camera is rolling. But TV crews and teams I have worked with have never given this much importance and this team was no exception. I made a few more attempts. Each time there was a disturbance and we had to cut, I could feel my temper sizzling.

I took a deep breath and said tiredly, smiling slightly despite the fatigue: 'I am sorry. I am tired, so I am getting easily distracted by the noise.'

That did the trick. The director yelled for floor silence and he got it. And I did my long introductory line in one take.

> **Note to self:** I am disciplined and almost always in control of the situation. I have to remember to extend the same discipline to my temper.

LIVING IN ANOTHER COUNTRY

While I have changed a little, my life has changed a lot over the past few years. I now live in the UK and work in both India and the UK. As my life continues to change, I try and adapt to the situation. Moving to the UK has meant that careerwise things have changed. My work in television in India has dwindled, my work in movies has increased somewhat and I am attempting to break into the British film and television industry.

Don't you love new beginnings? I typed that and paused ... for what else can a beginning be but new? I wondered if anyone thought of it that way. 'Same old beginning'. I don't think so. So – new beginnings. I love them. There is something about the excitement coupled with self-doubt that spurs me on.

After nineteen years of working before the camera in India, I came to England and decided to look for similar work. When I told my friends and family that I was going to see if I could work in two continents at the same time, my plan was met with scepticism. Except for my parents, Graham and Kripa, everyone looked at my enthusiasm rather dubiously. Oh, they didn't show it but I could hear them loud and clear: 'Poor Anu and her crazy ideas.' The ones that truly cared about me valiantly suppressed their instinct and came up with 'how exciting' and 'wow' and so on. The ones who thought they cared more said, 'it is very difficult to make it there' and 'you cannot hope to get work in film and television there'.

They were missing the point entirely.

I have always been someone who has enjoyed the process and not necessarily the destination. For instance, with the talk show I enjoyed the process of starting out as a nervous host and then becoming a host whom people wanted to talk to. I enjoyed the process of transformation more than the transformation itself. Partly because somewhere along the line people started seeing a me that wasn't there – made me out to be nicer than I was, more intelligent than I could be. But I knew how much I had learnt and that's also what I enjoyed.

And so it is here. I love the idea of going to an audition. After *Indira*, I have never been to one. I love the idea of having an agent. I have never had one. And I love the idea of doing a tiny, tiny role in some obscure TV series in the UK and then claiming to be the international star in the family. Technically speaking, that would be true, wouldn't it? Someone who has worked in an international project is an international star, right? So what if it was in a role where she ran around in the background with a hundred other people, screaming 'Oh god! Run for your lives! They are loose!'? (1. No, I haven't done that role – not yet. 2. I have thought about doing that in a zoo.)

I began with gusto. I got my website in place. I got two

young film-makers to shoot my showreel. I persuaded Graham to shoot my portfolio. And then I enrolled myself on a website and started applying to casting calls. And lo! Within a week I had an invite from three agencies to come and meet them. There were a few other calls for product promotions in supermarkets but I figured that wouldn't get me the title 'international star', so I ignored them. (Besides, my mum and dad wouldn't have thought twice about dragging me away by the ear if they caught me doing that. And even I am too old for some indignities.)

The first call was for an interview. A pretty young thing teetering on heels came to meet me at the very posh reception of Battersea Studios (not a very auspicious name for a beginning but it's still new, right?) and took me up to a glass-enclosed conference room with purple cushions. I couldn't decide what fascinated me more – the PYT on her six-inch heels miraculously navigating stairs or the sheer audacity of having purple cushions on a burgundy sofa.

While I was making up my mind, she started talking to me and I realized SHE was the one I was there to meet. So I dutifully handed over my CV and waited.

She read it and said, 'Nineteen years?'

'Yes,' I replied.

'Full time?'

'Yes.'

'Wicked!'

I stopped myself from saying, 'Not really. They think I am nice,' and then realized she meant it as a compliment (although she was bang on about my character).

Five minutes later, as I left with a call for audition in

my hand, I was almost skipping down the pavement. They wanted me to prepare two monologues and I knew I was going to have so much fun choosing and performing them. But would I be able to do it? Ooooh! Nervousness, self-doubt and excitement, my faithful companions who spur me on...

But I never knew how I would have done on those monologues. For the next agency I met had me do a reading and the very next day they wrote back saying they would like to represent me. I got thrilled that they were impressed but then I wondered if I was good enough. I wonder if there will be many auditions and I wonder if there will be as many rejections. There we go again – self-doubt and excitement...

> Note to self: It is not wrong to doubt your ability as long as it doesn't paralyse you. Sometimes self-doubt is the difference between trying hard and doing your best.

As much as my life has changed and continues to do so, one thing that hasn't changed is my ludicrous sense of humour. Let me tell you about the British choppers ... no, I am not talking about British serial killers, I am talking about the big whirly birds.

It was a lovely day in London. The temperature hovered at about 15 degrees and the sun made an occasional appearance, turning a pleasantly cold day into a warm one. I had just returned from playing pool with Graham (he was my fiancé then) and his friends during their lunch break. Saying I 'played' pool is something of an exaggeration. I still haven't figured out how to hold the cue. I am certain they are all horrified at my complete lack of pool skills and valiantly try to cover it but the occasional look of resigned horror passes fleetingly across their face and makes me chuckle. You see, another example of my ludicrous sense of humour. Anyone else would have tried hard to improve their game but not me. I'm sure I will get better as time goes by but I am not about to beat myself up for not being a pro in the first few attempts.

As I was walking down a quiet side street, I noticed two helicopters circling overhead. They made three passes. And the third time it seemed as though one of them changed course to fly directly above me. My shoelaces chose that exact moment to come undone and I went down on my haunches to tie them. When I stood up I noticed the other helicopter change its course.

What if it was the anti-terrorist squad and they had mistaken me for a terrorist? After all, I was wearing dark glasses, carrying a backpack, and was dressed in a black sweater, jeans and running shoes. Plus I had bent down to tie my laces just as the first chopper made its overhead pass. Would they consider it an evasive manoeuvre typical of a terrorist on his way to bombing a tube station?

I took a deep breath and continued walking, pooh-poohing the idea. I was just getting myself to calm down when one of the helicopters moved to hover about thirty feet directly above me. At that moment the street didn't seem like a very safe place for me to be. I looked up and saw a man dressed in black standing at the entrance to the chopper. My blessed short-sighted eyes couldn't make out what he held in his hand or where he was looking. I was beginning to panic but obviously there was no way I could outrun a chopper. I looked around for cover. I was getting into the mood quite nicely – I was sweating and the pounding of my heart was drowned only by the noise of the whirring blades. I knew there was nothing else I could do but walk away and walk I did, expecting a voice to yell any moment now over a hailer asking me to stop right where I was.

I let my imagination run away with me for a few more seconds and then my overactive imagination tripped and fell over on its face because the helicopter swerved away and landed somewhere in the school grounds, picked up someone and took off. My initial relief quickly gave way to sheepishness and now, as I narrate the incident, I am only left with amusement.

> **Note to self:**
> Allowing your imagination its ludicrous flights of fancy can be fun as long as you remember to have a good laugh at the end.

I am sitting in one of the innumerable parks in London as I write this. Around me is a curious mixture of modern and ancient buildings. Glass and brick and ugly lines coexist in harmony with gracious arches and Victorian facades. But in the end, like everywhere else, functionality triumphs over beauty. Older buildings that are not precious enough or useful enough to be preserved are pulled down frequently to be replaced by modern architecture.

How quick we are to get rid of the old. Be it buildings, traditions, values or even people. When a reporter asked me about culture and values and whether older ones were better than the ones that exist now, I could only draw a parallel to these buildings. If it is beautiful and gives joy to the beholder, by all means preserve it. But if it is structurally unsound, if the crumbling walls threaten to crush human life, then go ahead and raze it.

I suppose the intelligence is in being able to identify what needs to be preserved and what doesn't.

I thoughtfully nibbled on a strawberry as I looked at the people around me. All of them are dressed in working clothes – either black or blue. The women bring in a random splash of colour in this monotony of hues. Occasionally there is a man valiantly trying to break the stereotype with a pink shirt or a purple tie but such brave men are few and far between and the colour you see most in London during a working day is either dark blue or black.

And the politeness! You don't need to jostle and elbow your way to get into a bus or train. You don't have to worry about some pervert bumping into you on a crowded street. You don't have men staring at your neckline (and if they do, they are discreet about it). But you do have to mind your Ps and Qs. And you have to remember that you have to wait for your turn. Everywhere.

Take, for instance, the supermarket. If I am looking for, say, a prepaid card, I am used to walking up to the counter and, regardless of whether someone else is being served or not, asking if they have one. I am not asking her to give it to me if she does have one. If I know she has one I am quite happy to wait my turn. But I don't see the point in wasting time waiting if she doesn't have what I want. The first time I did that, the lady very politely told me, 'You will have to wait, ma'am. I am serving this customer here.' (the undertone clearly spelling: 'What kind of boor are you?') My first reaction was, haven't they heard of multi-tasking?

But gradually I realized that their approach reduces chaos.

On the roads, people actually give way. And they wave their hand in thanks when you pull your car to the side and give way to them. There are no wild attempts to overtake on the left or to sneak past you at the lights. If these do happen they are too infrequent for me to have spotted them. When you are walking, it is not unusual to have a passerby wish you good morning. The first time an old man smiled and greeted me as he walked past me, I was startled. I nervously walked away from him, thinking he was a weirdo. But when it happened more and more, I realized this was a custom and not an entirely unpleasant one.

On the train I am used to nudging past people as much as I am used to people pushing past me as they get out. But if you see an Englishman who is stuck behind someone who is needlessly blocking his way, eight out of ten times he will not push past. He will wait behind the person, fuming silently and rolling his eyes. I find this incredibly amusing as well as curious. (In Madras, the person in question would have been unceremoniously pushed aside.) As a result I have been forced to become more patient and polite myself.

They don't jump queues. On the flip side, they (sometimes aggravatingly) queue up for everything. I must confess I find it a very quaint trait. And as for the courtesy, I love it. Many a time men will allow a lady to precede them when getting on and off a bus or train.

At the gym where I work out, men hold the door open for me if they are coming out as I am going in. Earlier I used to hesitate and wait and generally act clumsy. But nowadays I sail through, thanking them for the courtesy. It is lovely pretending to be a lady instead of the rough tramp I usually am.

Even customer complaints are dealt with in a different manner. We bought a box of strawberries at the local cooperative supermarket and after we walked out I discovered that they were rotten. Normally I would hesitate to go back and tell them but when I summoned up my courage (it was after all six pounds – almost 500 rupees – and yes I still convert it into Indian money and get outraged at the prices) and went up to the supervisor, she said, 'Oh, sorry about that. Let me get you another box,' and she picked up a fresh box, checked the strawberries, handed the box to me and apologized again. I found the behaviour rather odd. She was neither subservient nor defensively arrogant. She was simply matter of fact. And I thought, What? I don't have to fight for my rights? Oddly enough, that left me quite deflated because I was all prepared to battle!

On the other hand, the distance that is slowly creeping into our cities in India has embedded itself firmly in the people here. There are no warm neighbourly visits. No one invites you home for tea or coffee (at least not as easily or as often as they do in India). When I speak to someone, their intonations and inflections give me a disoriented feeling – like I am watching a movie and they are speaking dialogues. Not for them, the highs and lows of the excited way we speak in India. It is not that they speak in monotone. But as a people, they appear more controlled. The much vaunted stiff upper lip, I suppose.

While there is much that I love about the English way of life, these are the things I miss here in England.

> **Note to self:** You can choose what you learn. I'd like to think that from England I take back to my Indian warmth the refreshingly cool blanket of politeness.

I could always go and find Indians and I would slip easily into familiar comfort. But I don't go to a new country so I can set up a mini India or a mini Madras. I go in the hope of absorbing from the people.

There are other things that I bring with me to my life in London – and some unlikely lessons too.

I am always complaining about the kind of drivers I have encountered in Madras – including earlier in this book. And I frequently say that if anything good comes out of driving amongst mad, crazy, inconsiderate drivers, I'll eat my hat!

After nearly twenty years of driving on Indian roads I had to repeat the whole L-plate process in order to get a licence here in the UK. I was quite miffed that I had to do it. After all, I had driven in Madras, Calcutta, Pune, Delhi and Mumbai and I was damned if I was going to be nervous about driving on English roads. But rules are rules so I decided to do what needed to be done.

I enrolled myself for driving classes and that's when I learnt that I had been doing everything wrong for the last twenty years. I am a confident driver and am used to steering with one hand with the other resting on the gear. I could even turn the wheel with the heel of my palm or flip my wrist so I was gripping the steering wheel from underneath. Just like a taxi driver. And when you think that I have driven all these years without a single accident, one would assume there wasn't anything terribly wrong with my driving.

But my British driving instructor disagreed, and quite vehemently. 'Your steering is atrocious,' was his response to what I thought was a pretty cool style of driving. Then he said I didn't check the mirrors often enough. And I didn't slow down enough and I didn't drive enough to the left. The list went on. At the end of the hour, I was so demoralized that I was driving worse than a learner driver.

I shifted gears jerkily, stuck too close to the left side of the road, nervously glanced in the mirrors too often and in general started moving at a far slower pace. And what response did that elicit? 'More gas! More gas!' my instructor yelled.

What was more frustrating was when I pointed out that most of the other drivers on the road did not hold the steering wheel properly, did not drive on the extreme left, did not check their mirrors every time they veered a few inches either way, my instructor's response was, 'Well, everyone reverts to their bad habits once they get their licence.'

So was he saying that I was going to have to unlearn everything just so I could get the licence and then I could revert to whatever the hell it was I called driving? Hmm, I wasn't sure if that was the right approach. After a few classes I decided to take a break. By now I had nearly maxed my theory test (yes, they do have a theory test as well as a practical test, and no, you cannot slip a few notes into the test instructor's hand and get your licence) and with my provisional licence I could drive as long as I had those dratted L plates and a fully qualified driver next to me.

Graham's parents' visit was a boon. Since mum was a qualified driver she could sit beside me (dad bravely sat at the back) and I could drive them wherever they wanted to go. A fine arrangement: they got to avoid public transport and I got to practice. Plus, since mum had seen me handle crazy traffic in Madras, she was confident about my ability to handle London traffic. The fact that she is unflappable in the car was an added bonus.

When we went for a short holiday to Norfolk, I got plenty of practice in the countryside. I was nervous and tense on empty roads – because I expected a buffalo or cow to dart out from the fields or some mad driver to zoom out of the side roads. Graham and his parents were relaxed because they knew it wouldn't happen. I, on the other hand, was more relaxed when I was on busy streets with cars driving bumper to bumper and pedestrians diving between cars to get to the other side. Funny, huh?

I was driving down a country road which was just wide enough for one car. I could feel the tension levels rise a bit when I had to reverse in order to pull into a passing place to let another car by. I was pretty calm as I did that and then I was on my way again. But tension levels shot through the roof a few minutes later when a car came roaring down a curve and ground to a halt a few feet away. My reaction? I grinned at the driver (who grinned back sheepishly), pulled over to the side and let him pass. And on one of the main roads, when a car suddenly backed out on to the road, everyone gasped while I calmly honked and moved out of the way after checking that it was safe for me to veer out of my lane.

See what I mean? I would like to learn what it is to be a good driver – technically speaking. But I would like to keep my nerves of steel and lightning reflexes (come on, allow me some of my illusions!) when it comes to driving. Having always been someone who likes to take away something good from every situation, I realized that it means I do have to thank our drivers for the above mentioned nerves of steel and quick reflexes.

I never thought the day would come... Just goes to show, what you are complaining about is actually teaching you a lesson. Time to eat my hat, I suppose.

So if you ask me if I like it here the answer is yes, indeed. But if you ask me if I have changed, well, yes and no. For if I am to try and apply all of these in India, I have to admit I'd probably get run over, trampled and left behind and find myself in all sorts of embarrassing situations. (Try saying Hi to a stranger on the road in India.) And as much as I enjoy it here amidst all the pleases and thank yous, I am equally comfortable in the delightful chaos that is my life in Madras. And I love the new facets to my identity that seem to keep getting forged as time goes by.

> **Note to self:**
> Sometimes the very things you complain about might be preparing you for something you never imagined you would have to face.

How many identities do we have? No, I am not talking about your voter ID, passport, driving licence, etc. I am talking about something more basic than that: nationality, region, gender, language, religion. How many of

> **Note to self:**
> Adapting to cultures is the best way to integrate. But adapting doesn't mean forgetting where you come from or losing your identity.

these do I emphasize? The answer: none. To me my identity is more than any one of these and more than the sum of these parts, which is why I can never relate to people who focus completely on being only Indian or only Tamil in any context. One cannot allow that to rule one's life. Somehow when you do that, you miss out on so much more.

While looking for a place to stay in London, some people were surprised that I chose not to look for a place that was predominantly occupied by Indians. I couldn't understand this logic. I already have that in Madras – my neighbours, family and friends. Why would I want to replicate that in London? Especially given that it's impossible?

Yet, around me, I see so many people clinging to their Tamilness or their Indianness. They live in closeknit communities and try to recreate their own little Delhi, Madras or Kolkata in a country that couldn't be more different.

Maybe I don't understand their point of view. Maybe I never will. But when you are in another country, why is it so hard for us to integrate? When we are distinct by nature, why do we try to highlight it by design?

I was sitting at a train station next to a young girl. From her skin tone, I could make out that she was Asian. Her clothes were totally Western but the content of her conversation was not. 'If I am fasting, I don't tell anyone. Else it won't work' – these words spoken in a broad London accent seemed so strange yet so typical of the multicultural society many countries have become.

I understand patriotism. I understand passion for Tamil as a language. But at what point does either become obsessive and misguided? We forget that the trademark of a Tamilian is the ability to receive and take care of guests (*virundhombal*), courtesy, kindness and warmth. Instead we focus on rituals and forgotten customs. We forget that the trademark of an Indian is hard work, perseverance and adaptability and focus instead on pulling out the racism card at the first sign of a difference of opinion.

And then there are those who wear their passion for Tamil as if it is the latest fashion trend. Behind their professed love for the language is an insincerity that is jarring. How come they love Tamil but haven't taken the trouble to learn to read the language? How come they love Tamil cinema but only those that are established hits? Why do they feel the need to scoff at the West in order to prove that their culture is better, richer and more vibrant?

But amongst all these are the true patriots and true lovers of Tamil culture. They are the ones who showcase India to people who are only too willing to appreciate its vibrant chaotic beauty. And these are the people I adore. They are comfortable in their own skin. They feel neither inferior nor superior. They treat every culture as their equal even as their pride in their heritage shines through. They don't need to mock another culture in order to prove the merits of their own. They are able to appreciate aspects of the Western culture without compromising on their essential Indianness or Tamilness.

As our country changes with the times, Indians abroad embrace the changed mishmash of traditions as essentially Indian and somewhere along the way the one thing they want to cling to tends to get lost.

I wonder if, as the years go by and I continue to shuttle between Madras and London, if I too will lose what is essentially Tamil or Indian? And for someone like me who has never focused on either aspect of her nature, how would I know when I lose it? And would it matter?

In school, I wore Western clothes and played basketball with the boys. I sang English songs, read English books yet I learnt Bharatanatyam and Carnatic music. I have acted in Tamil movies, I have run businesses, I love western cuisine and drool at the prospect of spicy biryani and shorshey maach (Bengali fish curry in mustard) I have been married, I have been divorced, I have married again, that too an Englishman. I don't have children and I don't want any. I live in London and I work in Madras. When you look at all this, how much of it is Indian? How much of it Tamil?

Note to self:
Trying to pin down your identity is like putting yourself into a box and missing out on many enriching experiences. As difficult as it might be, it is important to accept that your identity is a confusing smorgasbord of things.

More to the point – how much of it is important? Have I already lost parts of my identity? Or have I borrowed from different cultures to forge an identity entirely my own? I'd like to think that it is the latter. I am Indian. I am Tamil. I am a woman. But I am also other things. After all, to me my identity is more than any single one of these and more than the sum of these parts.

I have learnt that as life changes, it means also that one has to be more open than one is used to usually being.

I have been told that I have a great imagination. It is not as much of an advantage as people make it out to be. You see, when you have a great imagination, your mind works out all kinds of possibilities and you start to wonder if it is safe to walk across to the nearest grocery store.

Thankfully I am more of a warrior than I give myself credit for, so invariably I overrule unjustified fears. Even if a small voice continues to lurk at the back of my mind insistently whining about all the things that could go wrong.

And so it was when I got an email from someone called 'Milad Latoof' asking me if I would like to play a role in an Arabic short film. My first thought was: 'How safe is it to meet a stranger?' My next worry was that the middle-east is not exactly a bastion of women's lib. I thought about it for a bit and decided to take it forward. After all, it is not often that someone like me gets such an opportunity. In fact, if Kripa were to hear about this, her response would be 'You go, girl!'

Plus, if I proceeded with caution, maybe it would be a great experience. And if, after going to the film location, I discovered he was a potential rapist, I could probably kick him where it hurts most and run away screaming.

With this reassuring and practical plan of action, I agreed to do the project. Milad asked if we could speak on the phone. When we did, and I realized that Milad was female, I felt a sense of relief. It was a female director so I didn't need to worry, did I? Then that insistent voice piped up: 'What if it is a woman fronting for someone else?' Then again, so many women from the middle-east long to speak for their sisters. If I didn't support them, how different was I from the men who were supposedly their oppressors?

That argument convinced me to accept the role. The location was a good hour and a half away from where I lived in London and as I traipsed off it occurred to me that I was better off wearing my running shoes, just in case.

I was met at the station by Aleana, a young girl from Russia, and once again I felt relief. This was just a young girl. My usual sense of adventure bolstered my courage as we trudged off to the house where we were to film.

As we reached, I saw a man waiting outside and I looked curiously at him. Aleana said, 'This is Milad's father.' The man smiled at me and gave me an assessing look that made me stiffen. Then he wished us good luck with the filming, got into his car and drove off. I might be wrong but that certainly looked like a father making sure his daughter was safe – from ME!

Ironic, isn't it? Here I was worrying about my safety and there was a father waiting to make sure I was not some weirdo before leaving his daughter and her friends in my company. I suppose I must have looked fairly unthreatening for him to decide in a few seconds that I was not a potential threat. Odd, considering I was wearing jeans, jacket, running shoes and carrying a backpack – a description, I am told, that fitted the London Tube Bomber. Maybe my wonderfully kind and gentle personality, along with all the other things I am not, shone through brightly enough to reassure him.

That was the point where I relaxed completely. I walked into the house

> **Note to self:** Being open to new opportunities does not mean throwing caution to the winds.

and met the team. The director, Milad, was Iraqi. There was a Russian producer, a Spanish cinematographer and sound technicians and a Syrian fellow actor. And then there was me, good old Anu Hasan from India. You can't get more international than that!

I was delighted to work with this young group of individuals who obviously knew what they were doing. Milad impressed me with her vision, the cinematographer with his competence and Aleana with her ability to remain unflappable as she ran around organizing details pertaining to production. These kids already knew more than half of what I had taken fifteen years to learn. Thankfully I did know a little more than they did – a fact that reassured my not inconsiderable professional ego. I even got to speak two lines in Arabic – although the Syrian actor burst out laughing when I said one of the lines. I was miffed and wondered if I should ask him to repeat a *thirukkural* after me. But I decided to be magnanimous and forgive him –after all, isn't that one of the things I have learnt in all these years that I have worked?

As the day drew to a close, I was left feeling wonderfully happy. Not for a job well done but for such a promising group of youngsters. When Milad told me she was going to submit her short film to the Dubai and Abu Dhabi film festivals as well as Hollyshorts (the Hollywood short film festival), Edinburgh Film Festival and Cambridge Film Festival, I was delighted at her ambition and enthusiasm.

And every experience leaves me marvelling at how the times are a-changing – and the women with it.

I was filming in a grocery store in north London and two

girls who were working in the store ran up to meet me. Their excitement was contagious as they chattered away, telling me how thrilled they were to see me. I sensed there was more to their exuberance than meeting an actress and I was right. They missed home – meaning they missed speaking in Tamil. Although they were surrounded by Tamil speakers, it wasn't the Tamil they were used to in Tamil Nadu and that was what was giving them more pleasure – hearing me speak regular, unaccented Tamil.

This in itself is an indication of how grounded they were. They were thrilled to see me but were not in awe of me. I asked them where they were from and they named a village near Trichy. Surprised, I asked them why they had chosen to come and work in a grocery store in London. The girls smiled at me and said, 'Oh, we didn't come here to work. We came here to study. I am doing a Master's in telecommunication and my sister is doing a Master's in computer application. We are just working to contribute to our college tuitions.'

These girls worked three days a week in the grocery store and three days a week in KFC and went to college during the day. When I asked them how the people in their village reacted to that, the elder one answered wryly, 'Well, we do have people who think that a school teacher's daughters should not work in a store like this. But we don't care. If we didn't do this our father would have a larger financial burden and we don't want that.'

I felt like standing up and applauding them. I felt strangely proud to meet young girls who understand that there is dignity in labour and that it is a matter of pride to contribute to expenses. I have always wondered why we are so reluctant to accept that work is work. I know quite a few people who, in order to save face, would rather stay at home unemployed than do some work that seems beneath their dignity. They suffer from what I call the 'what will people say' syndrome. But I have also seen people sneering at someone who is not doing what according to them is a 'decent' job.

I have come across that attitude myself. Especially after I did that commercial. A cinematographer who wanted me to work in his feature film to be shot in London said, 'I saw that you've done commercials for the local business. You know, if you are working in this movie, you have to be more selective about commercials.' Meaning these commercials were beneath my dignity. The poor man didn't expect my response, which was: 'If I am going to be working in your movie, you will have to understand that you cannot tell me what to do when it comes to my personal decisions about work.' The haste with which he back-pedalled would have been amusing if I weren't so irritated with his attitude. Why do we assume that some work is below our dignity and some work isn't?

In London I have seen the vice-president of a big company working at the reception of a golf club because he wanted to take it easy. It is so liberating to see that no one looks down on him for what he is doing. I see actors who have done large projects willingly work as extras in another, simply for the experience, and no one treats them like dirt unlike the production managers and assistant directors in India who treat the extras like they are somehow beneath them. I don't understand why we treat people according to their station in life, why the class system seeps into every aspect of our lives.

So the British have their own class system. But I still feel sad when I see that the senseless class system still lives on with the immigrants in the UK. I would have expected people to shed prejudices and biases when starting afresh. Obviously it is more difficult than I make it out to be.

> **Note to self:** There are many things about our culture I want to retain ... but the class system is not one of them.

I have recently discovered that I get an incredible amount of joy when I work on the land. I have always wanted to retire early and become a farmer. But never having actually done farming work I had a niggling doubt about whether I would be able to handle it.

Close to where we live in London is a park called The Tarn. It has a lovely lake in the middle surrounded by four acres of wooded area. I often go there for a solitary lunch, read my book or just gaze at the Muscovy ducks and Canadian geese. On one of my trips I saw a notice saying they were looking for volunteers and I immediately signed up, thereby becoming the youngest member of The Friends of The Tarn.

When I mentioned that I volunteered at the local park, one of the men I was working with in a film project in the UK said, 'You come from a respectable family. Why do you have to do this?' I felt a flash of irritation. If I had come to seek asylum from a war-torn country, I would have certainly shown some gratitude to the country I now called home and tried to integrate and contribute as much as I could in return. And I certainly wouldn't live on welfare. But his bias is his baggage and I suppose some baggage is much harder to shrug off than others. Thankfully it isn't too difficult for me to shrug off such cultural bias with respect to volunteer work.

Note to self: If you feel good about something you do, what others say about it should not determine whether you enjoy doing it or not.

When I signed up as a volunteer, I was warmly welcomed into the group. Apparently the council did not have enough funding to maintain The Tarn, so this group had been formed in order to preserve the park for future generations. I liked the sound of that.

I realized on the first day that I knew very little about gardening. You can't blame me. I had never gardened until now and I didn't know what tools were used for what. You had to use a fork to turn the soil over, the leaves needed a rake, the unruly hedges a secateur, shears or the loppers. The list was endless. But slowly I learnt how to use these tools and I was soon wielding them with a comfort that surprised even me. In fact, sometimes, the rest of the team would come to me for help with chopping off a branch or uprooting a particularly difficult bramble bush.

The Tarn is serene and almost magical. There is a bit of land on the other side of a canal and the only way to reach it is to put a ladder across the canal and place a wooden plank over the rungs, then tie a rope to a tree on either end of the canal and walk across the shaky bridge holding the rope for support. The first time I saw them do it I was almost beside myself with excitement. Bob asked me if I would be okay walking across and almost before he completed his sentence, I had bounded across grinning happily. I saw him roll his eyes as if to say, 'I should have known.'

Being the youngest meant that I was quickly clubbed with the men when it came to the hard work. If you ask my friends from BITS they will tell you this has always been the case. Steve once said to me, 'Anu, are you going to be in next Thursday? Bob isn't coming and I need help putting up the bridge. The women can't do it.' I started smiling at the familiar pattern.

A day of volunteering means backbreaking work – sawing overhanging branches and chopping them down to smaller bits, putting them into rubbish bags and hauling them away for the council to dispose of. It also means turning over the soil, cutting invasive ivy roots, planting trees and raking dead leaves. But the best part of the day is when we all come back from our respective areas in the park for afternoon tea. Hot-cross buns with cheese and coffee or tea served with lots of teasing and gentle ribbing. Jenny sometimes brings in homemade fruit cake and I take the occasional apple cake or gobi paranthas.

I love every minute I spend there. It's a win-win situation. The park gets volunteers to maintain it so that more people can enjoy it, and I feel that I am doing something good. I learn more about the land and how to care for it. Most importantly, I am getting incredibly fit. Try chopping wood and hauling six bags that weigh about thirty kilos for a distance of 50 metres and you will know what I am talking about. And on the days I work at The Tarn, I never have to count the calories. Six hours of work there means I can pretty much eat any damned thing I want!

I wonder why I have never done this in India ... but wait, I have! When I was about ten, my friends Ammu, Thanga, Viji and I formed a society called Happy Society. The aim was to do the gardening work for the people on our street, get paid for it and use that money for something good. We even had our own bank account which Ammu's mother had opened for us.

We earned two rupees for cleaning someone's garden. When we had collected enough money we went across to the construction workers in the street behind ours and gave their kids slates, notebooks and pencils. We worked on Saturdays and held Sunday meetings for which our mothers made us custard and cake and other yummies to eat.

Happy Society had such a romantic view of the world. I smile now when I think about those days. Credit also goes to our mothers who encouraged us to actually go work on someone else's garden despite popular opinion in the eighties that it was below one's dignity to do such work. We were so happy doing what we were doing.

And now, more than thirty years later, here I am in London doing pretty much the same thing – hanging out with nice people, working hard on someone else's garden and taking a break to eat scrumptious stuff. Happy Society lives on in spirit with Ammu, Thanga and Viji having been replaced by Carole, Bob, Steve and Jenny.

It is funny how history repeats itself. I just didn't expect it to do so in my own lifetime.

MEMORIES

The mention of Happy Society drew my attention to memories and I decided I cannot finish this book without dedicating a chapter to them.

I smile when I think of how I have lived my life. So many changes. When you move on in life you tend to think that what you have left behind remains unchanged, staying exactly the same as it is in your memory. But of course that isn't the case.

A few months ago I went back to Trichy. Our old house had been pulled down and a new one built in its place. The new house bore absolutely no resemblance to the house I grew up in. What is surprising is that the decision to pull down a house that held so many memories was made in a very practical manner. There was frequent flooding, the house had to be razed – ergo, this one had to go and a new one had to be built.

Neither of my parents felt hesitant about making this choice. While it would be understandable coming from me or my brother (considering both of us left the house to go to college and never went back to live there long-term), I was surprised that my mother, who I have always thought of as sentimental, coolly gave the go ahead to my father. I suppose the nuisance of having to clean up mud and filth after every flooding was enough to wipe away any emotional attachment she had built over the years.

When I spoke about my upcoming visit to my friends, most of their responses implied that I was going to feel at least a little sad when I saw physical proof that the house I had grown up in was really gone. They reminded me of the old adage: you never miss something until you lose it. So it was with some trepidation that I planned my first visit to the 'new' house.

It was a marvelous piece of work. The house somehow manages to create the illusion of being palatial despite being built on the same area that the old house stood on.

As I stepped in for the first time, I paused – waiting for the pang of nostalgia that never came. What happened to the memory of playing in the dining room while my mother cooked? Maybe the fact that the pressure cooker exploded during one such occasion made it a less desirable memory. What about the memory of swinging from the doorway beam? Maybe the fact that I slipped and landed on my chin and had to live with a distorted chin for almost a week made it a memory that was better forgotten. And what about the garden where I first learnt to cook over a wood fire? Maybe the fact that I discovered the microwave and modern implements that made cooking less tiresome made that memory less treasured?

I walked from one room to another, expecting to be assaulted by nostalgia, and felt nothing but admiration for this beautiful new building that had seamlessly replaced my family home.

I walked up the staircase and stopped short.

As a child I grew up on a steady diet of Enid Blyton. By the time I was in the first standard, I had graduated to Jack Higgins, Alistair McLean and so on. I think I started understanding what I was reading when I was in the fourth. I remember the smell of books in the upstairs cupboards. I remember my indignation when one of our relatives borrowed some books and didn't return them. I remember a summer project where I neatly labelled and catalogued all the books in our 'library' only to have the said relative come and turn my library into disarray.

The smell of books. That hadn't changed at all. Before me were rows and rows of books that my father had collected on his travels. I pulled out a book at random. It was a Robert Ludlum. *The Holcroft Covenant*. On the first page, in my father's handwriting I read: '13 Oct 1986 – Bombay Airport.' The smell of the books and those words written in my father's precise handwriting brought the nostalgia crashing in. I looked around me and without volition, my mouth curved into a smile.

There's that cupboard of unread books that my father has kept aside. These books he has not read. He says that he will start reading them when he retires. This cupboard has more serious subjects – philosophy, theology, the Vedas and so on. On another shelf are encyclopaedias, volumes about crime and punishment and even DIY books. The rest of the shelves are stocked with suspense, thrillers and murder mysteries.

I was surprised to see sixteen volumes of *Children's Hour* nestling in a corner. These red hardbound books were a personal favourite of mine when I was in school. Some volumes were more worn than others. Volume two was almost in tatters – but that was understandable because it was titled *Favourite Fairy Tales*. So was the volume titled *Leaders and Heroes*. My smile widened at this clear indication of my once budding personality. I must confess I haven't changed much.

My eyes travelled across the shelves and I spotted my own contribution to my father's collection, splashes of colour between the sombre blacks and browns. Bright blue Mills & Boons. Red Harlequin romances. Lavender and White romances. I remember how startled my father was when I started reading them. Sometimes I think there was even a tinge of disappointment. He never understood my fascination for romance. He still doesn't but that's another story.

As I stood smiling at the thousand-odd books before me, I realized I was looking at the library that had shaped my attitude, moulded my language and captured my imagination for more years than I could remember. Before me was the road map that I had followed all these years. Happy endings. Thrilling chases. Sweeping romances. Everything that I had wanted in my life and everything that had been given to me – either in the form of real-life experiences or reel-life ones.

As I left the room, I was fiercely glad that this part of the house had

> **Note to self:**
> Change might make you uncomfortable but if you look hard enough at the change that is for the better, you will notice the still familiar things that offer you a measure of comfort.

not changed. They say you never appreciate something until you lose it. I never want to lose this because I couldn't appreciate it more.

My memories of my apartment in Madras are varied. This was the apartment I lived in for almost seven years and it had seen major changes in my life. I went from being married to divorced and broke to being single and successful and married again.

There have been some constant factors too and when it was time to part from some of them... Parting is sweet sorrow but there is nothing sweet about parting when you know you will never be together again. My love affair with the object of my affection had gone on for seven glorious years and in those years I have been very happy. I had complete reliability, comfort and freedom.

Ask Linda Goodman about the Cancer-Scorpio equation and she will rave about it. I am a Cancerian and the Scorpio in question... You thought I was talking about a man, didn't you? Well, if my Scorpio were a man I would have fallen irrevocably in love with it. Think about it – big-built, dark and handsome, stable and reliable and completely unintimidated by others. Isn't that the stuff M&B heroes are made of?

To me, my car has been the symbol of many things. At a time in my life, when I had no other assets, my Scorpio was the only thing I at least part owned.

When I look back, I see how incredibly lucky I was. I got opportunities beyond my wildest dreams. As I threw myself into work with enthusiasm (I know no other way) I built my asset base slowly and steadily.

It's a good thing I didn't care a hoot about my image and wearing designer clothes and buying expensive jewellery. It is this attitude that funnelled all my earnings into sensible investments instead of being frittered away partying or buying unnecessary things. Thank goodness for good old middle-class sensibility.

I still remember when I paid my final EMI on the car. I walked down to where the Scorpio was parked and patted and stroked it. (Unobtrusively, of course. The people in my apartment block already suspect that I am a little off my rocker. I didn't want to prove them right.)

I have some wonderful memories associated with my Scorpio. I have driven my father around in it. At first he clung nervously to the door handle until he was sure that I really was comfortable driving it. I have driven my mother around. I recall her beaming pride, which said, 'Look, my daughter drives a Scorpio!' I remember my nephew Nanda asking me '*Chithi*, why do you drive a lorry?' And I remember long drives with friends to Mudaliarkuppam, picnics by myself at secluded spots, errands, silly races with stupid men on the road. The list is endless.

And now the time had come for us to part ways. I lived in London now and came down only for film shoots. And since keeping a car unused is the best way to run it down to scrap, my father advised that I sell it.

I surprised even myself with the intensity of my resistance to the idea. After much persuasion from my father I reluctantly agreed and the search for an owner commenced. I refused to sell it to a stranger because who knew how they would treat my darling? When one of my friends told me his cousin was interested in buying my car, I decided to inspect him. After all, he had to treat my car well and handle it the way I used to. My mother teased me for acting as though I was giving my daughter's hand in marriage. Close enough.

That day when I took the car across, I could see at once that he liked it. Perhaps I am biased but what's there to dislike about my dark, gleaming monster? I wanted to see how he drove, so I pretended I didn't have a ride to the airport and since he was someone I knew, I asked him to drop me off with the car. I told him he could drop back the car at my friends' and leave the key there.

I observed him surreptitiously. Smooth gear changes – check. Right gear to engine ratio – check. Proper grip on steering wheel – check. Good judgement – check. Okay, he was good enough. And when he commented how smoothly the car ran, I swelled with pride.

We agreed on a price. I already had two other offers that were higher but I wasn't tempted to go with one of those instead. My car had to go to a good home; that was more important.

It was a pity that in between the time we agreed on the price and the exchange, some kids decided to use a nail to display their alphabetical prowess on the bonnet and side panels. When my watchman called to inform me, I almost cried. He himself was close to tears, which I found mildly amusing.

There was no way I was going to send my car out looking like that. And so, like a bride getting a facial before her big day, my car went in for some painting and body work.

Expensive, but thankfully my insurance took care of that little blip.

I told the buyer that he could collect my Scorpio from the garage after the body work had been done. I did not want to see my beautiful beast looking even more radiant than before and have to endure giving it away. Who knows, I might end up changing my mind and keeping it. So I was brave and strong and let it go. For I knew that everything that the Scorpio symbolized to me was still mine. I was still free. I could go where I wanted. And I had other assets that were proof of the path that I had successfully navigated.

> **Note to self:** Know when your attachment to something or someone is symbolic.

But you still have to agree – parting is not sweet sorrow.

My apartment too is fraught with memories. I have come back fatigued from work and fallen asleep immediately. I have spent many days lazing about. I remember one of those days when I had little else to do other than write and hang about at home. One of my friends was chatting with me and decided to drop in for some coffee. I am always raving about the coffee I make – of course, I rave about everything I do but that's another matter. I had bought fresh coffee beans only a few hours ago so I had that covered. I ran out to buy some pastries and came back and waited for him.

The evening began on an amusing note. My friend had said he would be there at five. I sat on the sofa reading a book. I knew it was five but I also knew he wasn't going to be here on time. At twenty past I got up and walked to the balcony. I had a feeling he was a few minutes away or maybe

I was just tired of waiting. I looked down and the watchman indicated that my friend was on his way up.

I walked to the door and opened it just as he was reaching to ring the bell. He was visibly startled and I was obviously delighted. I love startling people. The same does not apply to me, as you will soon find out.

He sauntered into the kitchen and watched me prepare the coffee. I make a big production of it. I grind the beans and carefully measure the powder into the percolator, make my guest choose a cup and then pour the decoction, milk and sugar into it in exact quantities. Even if I didn't do it this carefully the coffee would probably taste the same but I am not admitting that to anyone.

We sat at the dining table with our coffee cups and had been chatting for a couple of hours when I suddenly saw his eyes shift to a spot behind my shoulder. I tensed but have too much ego to show just how chicken I am. So I pretended not to notice. After a few more glances, he leaned forward and said in a low voice, 'Anu, you do know that there is something in the house, don't you?'

I knew exactly what he was talking about. Whenever I get scared I feel that I am not alone in the house. That presence is called fear. I remembered my cousin telling me the same thing – that something was watching her from a particular spot in the corridor. And there had been a few instances when I thought I had seen movement in the spot she was talking about. A trick of light, I told myself. Well, I better tell myself that. I live alone and I have no intention of believing otherwise. It's called survival.

My friend was watching me closely. I wondered how he

could use almost the same words and look at the same spot that my cousin had pointed out to me. I decided to come clean. I told him about the incident with my cousin. And he said, 'It has been watching me since I came in. I believe in djinns, and I think it's a djinn.' My skin crawled at that point because I too felt that we were not alone but I hid my fear behind a cheerful smile and said 'Okay, let it be there then. It won't do anything,' and we continued talking. After a few minutes he looked at me and said, 'It's gone now.' I tentatively tried to sense how the house felt and it did feel empty.

We continued talking for another hour and the conversation veered towards dogs. I walked across to my laptop to show him a picture of my dog. The living room was in semi-darkness save for the light that spilled over from the dining room where we had been sitting. The light from the computer screen feebly lit another portion of the room.

My friend walked behind me and I bent over my laptop to open the folder and smiled in delight at the picture of Shogun. I turned with the smile still on my face and froze. My friend was looking at me and in the half light, the face I was looking at was not the one I had been speaking to for the past few hours!

I took a step back shakily, swallowing my panic. He smiled and I felt my stomach clench in fear. I knew my grip on this façade of calm was tenuous at best. I decided to go for broke. 'Move into the light,' I said. He smiled again. With rising panic in my voice, I repeated, 'Move into the light, man. Your face has changed.' He stepped into the light and I was relieved to see the same face that I had been speaking to before.

He asked me what the matter was. Any other person would have ended the conversation, said a polite goodbye and seen him out of the house and probably run across to spend the night at a friend's place. But not me. People like me, we like to prod a snarling lion. 'Go back to the same place,' I told him. I watched as the light cast different shadows on his face.

I saw fear flit across his face as he said half-jokingly, 'Now you've scared me, Anu.' I laughed lightly, fine actress that I am. We came back and sat at the dining table and he looked over my shoulder at the spot in the corridor and said, 'It's back again now.' My imagination was on overdrive. Possession, evil spirits, djinns – I had had enough.

Part of me wanted to run out and part of me wanted to continue talking because it had been years since I had had such a nice time talking to someone about everything and nothing in particular. When he decided to go home it was almost midnight. A voice inside me said maybe it was best he left before midnight because who knew what might happen at the stroke of midnight?

I ignored the voice and bid him goodnight. As I gave him a quick hug and sent him on his way, his voice floated up from the stairs: 'Crap, man! There is no light on the stairs!'

'Do you want me to come down with you?' I called out.

His male ego responded, 'Naaah! I'll go home. I'll be fine. You scared me with that talk of changing face and all that.'

I closed the door behind his fading voice and turned to face my empty house which didn't feel empty. I paused and collected myself.

In all the years I have lived in this house, I have never felt unsafe here. At that particular moment, though, I wished I believed in God. Then I could have told myself that God would protect me. But it was too short a time to change a lifetime of beliefs. I resorted to logic.

Let me see now. I have lived alone in this house for four years. I have had several companions in that period – fear, disappointment, joy, depression, excitement. Each has taken a form almost tangible. They all come and go, but nothing stays. I have a saying that I use very often and I took comfort in that. 'This too shall pass.' Even if this was a trick of light.

> **Note to self:** We cannot explain some things ... the question is ... do we need to?

I slept with the lights on.

When I think about it now, I wonder if most of it wasn't our imagination. In fact, even my friend seems like part of my imagination – I had actually forgotten his name and had no idea where he was until he recently connected with me on Facebook, you know, the one place where you can store your memories and build new ones.

Recently I did something else to refresh old memories – I attended the reunion of the BITS batch of 1988 which took place in January 2013.

Going to BITS Pilani was one of the best decisions in my life. Never mind that it was because I thought I was a genius (a myth that was quickly dispelled) and because I loved the fibreglass basketball boards. It was a place where I made friendships that have lasted twenty-five years and counting.

My memories of college have grown hazy with time and I was looking forward to see how many others were in the same boat as me. Quite a few. I was also surprised to see how many people remembered stuff I had no clue about.

One of my friends reminded me how I had once saved his life. Exaggerating, I thought, but then he described a trip to a hill fort and told me how he had been walking on the edge of the wall and had slipped. Apparently I reached out, grabbed his belt and pulled him back in the nick of time, saving him from a twenty-feet drop. I have no recollection of this. While part of me panicked at the glaring evidence of the onset of dementia, another part reassured me that I was following the principles of the Bhagavad Gita – do something good and forget about it. Some consolation, that.

As I saw faces I hadn't seen in years, I felt a rush of happiness. Never mind the fading memories, we were building new ones on the strength of those. Everyone in that room that day had done well for themselves – there were CEOs, entrepreneurs, angel investors, investment advisors, departmental heads, designers and among all those highly accomplished men and women, an actress. We were like kids back in a playground and it was such a joy to know that you were accepted for what you were and not what you had accomplished.

Note to self: Make the effort to stay in touch with your friends ... as you grow older you will appreciate their presence in your lives much more.

Long after the reunion is over, the Facebook page continues to serve as our playground.

APPEARANCE AND
IMAGE

I must have been about seventeen when I became aware of this Stranger. She seemed to get along with everyone so well. They looked charmed and happy, those beautiful people. I longed to be her friend too and wished I could belong to that elite circle. But it was infra dig for me to admit to it openly. So I tried approaching her from another direction.

I wanted to be noticed so I gave some serious thought to my clothes. Tina Munim looked pretty cool with that wide leather belt over her shirt, maybe I would too. In an attempt to impress the Stranger, I spoke to my aunt and got her to buy me a white leather belt. I borrowed my father's shirt, wore it over pale cream trousers and cinched the belt tightly around my waist, which was none too slender even then.

I strutted into school and I remember everyone staring curiously at me. They didn't seem impressed. I was interested in only one person's reaction but the Stranger ignored me. I wanted to go up to her and ask her to teach me to be more like her but pride held me back. Thankfully there were other things that I was good at and I decided to bury the Stranger's non-acceptance under my other brilliant achievements.

After all, my athletic and intellectual abilities outshone most other things. Or did they?

I mentioned this to my mother and she was indignant. She told me, 'Never pay importance to appearances. Being a good person is more important than being a stylish and beautiful one. Don't compete with them.' Her words mollified me somewhat and I got over the Stranger's rejection easily enough.

Which is why when I realized that we had got into the same college, I wasn't too ruffled. I knew I could do nothing to impress her. And the need to do so slowly waned as I found other interests. My love for basketball was rekindled, my joy in acting took up a lot of my spare time and there were other things of earth-shattering importance – like impressing boys by showing them I was as strong as they were, proving I wasn't a sissy by diving off the stage expecting six of my mates to catch me … you get the picture.

And so college life went by with the Stranger and me avoiding each other. Sometimes I thought she looked rather silly. Very few people were willing to come right out and say that. They worried about being excluded from the elite circle. Slowly I stopped watching her. For a few years after I graduated from college I didn't come across her at all or perhaps I was too busy to notice her. A movie, a marriage, a start-up, a divorce – all these things were milestones in my life and I stumbled along.

I forgot about her, until one day my ex-father-in-law casually remarked that if there were an award for the world's worst-dressed female I would get it. I was hurt by the comment and turned to my ex-husband and his mother for support, but they looked anxious and shook their heads, warning me not to start an argument. And so the one thing that has always stood me in good stead came to my rescue again – my pride. I smiled blandly at everyone and excused myself from the table as soon as it was polite to do so.

Sitting on the bed, I wondered what I could have done to have avoided that comment and my mind wandered back to when I first set eyes on the Stranger. I bet if *she* had been the daughter-in-law, she would not have invited remarks of this kind. I wished I had made more of an effort to befriend her. Maybe she would have taught me a thing or two.

Years later, when I came back to acting and the tabloids decided I was newsworthy, pictures of me started appearing in magazines and newspapers. I was almost always dressed in fairly regular clothes while others around me were sleek and stylish. I noticed the Stranger in some of the pictures but she stayed away from me. She seemed to shine and I wondered if she would overshadow me. But when I looked at the pictures, my happy face seemed to outshine her elegant looks – at least in my eyes. I appreciated that it was great to have someone like her around. I admired her but I was no longer concerned about being accepted by her.

I remember one occasion vividly. For a brief moment our eyes met and she smiled at me, and I thought I might just get into her elite circle. I had, after all, paid some attention to my hair and clothes. But that was a one-off instance and my focus on running, Kalari and the like resurfaced. I seemed to disgust her and she drifted away.

I enjoyed the fleeting connection but in order to belong to her world, I was going to have to change everything I rejoiced in within my world. I loved feeling the wind in my face, the exhilaration of a run, being active. I loved being me and while I knew that if I really wanted to, I could be like the Stranger, I didn't have any enthusiasm left over to make the effort after I had chased all these other things that I loved.

I, therefore, have come to accept the inevitable. Our paths may occasionally cross but we shall never walk beside each other for any extended period of time. She belongs to a different world. I am sure you have met her. Most people call her Fashion.

> **Note to self:**
> Accept that while some qualities are mutually exclusive, if you are smart you can toggle between your choices.

I have never been svelte or skinny. If someone was asked to describe me they would probably use words like healthy, athletic, large, etc. Although I am quite happy with it, I know how much of an effort I make in order to be fit and healthy.

You see, my enthusiasm for cooking is only surpassed by my enthusiasm for food itself. I love food. Anyone who knows me well knows how my face lights up at the mention of food. And boy, can I pack it.

Naturally the flipside of such a love is that managing my weight is a constant battle. Everything was fine until last year. I could eat what I wanted and I would simply burn it off during my Kalari classes and runs. Happy days!

But being diagnosed as a hypothyroidic put an end to that. With TSH levels shooting through the roof, my slower metabolism combined with my undiminished love for food set me on a path of unprecedented weight gain.

It took many kilometres of walking and carefully planned binge sessions to get my weight back under control. Naturally, me being me, I wanted to bring it lower than it was when I started to gain weight. Maybe it is because I constantly want to know what I CANNOT do. That was a silly challenge I set myself.

I didn't start this topic to talk about my weight issue but about the issue of handling other people when it came to this.

It was interesting to see the reactions of other people. My family didn't bother about the weight gain except to tell me not to starve or overdo the exercising. While the former was unlikely, they knew the latter was a distinct possibility. My close friends urged me to be patient and slowly work my way back to my usual weight. But reactions in the outer circle were very odd.

Everyone seemed to take great relish in pointing out the obvious. While some did it subtly and gently, others approached the topic with just about as much sensitivity as a bull in a china shop.

The most offensive comment came from someone I thought was a friend. His first comment after not seeing me for more than three months was not 'How are you' or 'so long since I saw you' but 'What is this, akka? You have put on layers of lard!' Said in Tamil, it sounds very rude, not to mention crude. My instinctive retort was, 'I did it especially so you would have something to comment about.' Needless to say, our friendship ended at that point.

My retorts varied from sarcasm to outright indignation. And oddly enough, their reaction was indignation too.

They couldn't fathom why I was being rude to them.

Each time I snapped, you know the cycle – I ended up feeling guilty. And then I realized I was going about it the wrong way. These offensive reactions were coming from people who really didn't matter. Nice to have them around but I wouldn't die if they weren't there.

So I changed tack. The next time someone rudely pointed out that I had become fat, my response was 'Thank you' and I smiled sweetly. It was very funny to see their reaction. Bewilderment, followed by suspicion, followed by an embarrassed huff of laughter. All in quick succession. Most people stopped at that point and changed the subject, simply because they didn't know what else to say. But some persisted. They would say something along the lines of 'What, you have stopped working out now that you are married, is it?' Ah, indisputable logic – and one that I never understood. What has being married got to do with whether I would work out or not? It is not as if I am going to turn into a doormat or a baby-making machine. I am too old for both, thankfully.

My response to that particular attempt to continue Anu-bashing was 'Nope' and another sweet smile. That usually put paid to that line of conversation. After a point I started looking forward to people commenting about my weight. The more amused I got, the less stressful it was for me. At this point I would like to go on record that I would advocate this approach to anyone who gets stressed when other people are rude about their weight.

Now, after a year of struggling to find what works for this hypothyroidic body of mine, I have brought my weight somewhat under control but I am almost missing those encounters I used to have.

This morning some people I met at the YMCA exclaimed about how fit I was looking and how I had not changed a bit. I couldn't resist the impulse. I piped up, 'Oh, you should have seen me four months ago. I weighed 81 kilos.' The look of horror on their faces was satisfying. And I am vain enough to admit that the renewed flow of compliments was satisfying too.

But again, me being me, I decided to push my luck. I said, 'I now weigh 75 kilos. I still have 4 kilos I want to lose.' I could see their eyes running up and down and finally settling on my still comfortably-sized midriff. And they didn't disappoint me.

'Yes, you do need to lose more weight. All said and done, it is after marriage, isn't it? Not easy,' said one of them with a very wise look on his face. Inside me, a voice went, Huh? What? But I didn't give into my urge to come back with an acidic retort. I had been asking for it. I just said, 'Thank you,' and I smiled. No one understood why I did it. Neither did I, for that matter.

Working before the camera means you end up seeing yourself critically all the time. On the flipside, you also have to get used to being a 'celebrity'. I have always disliked this term. It

Note to self: Don't forget that other people's opinions do not define who you are. You do.

implies a transience I want no part of. I have seen many so-called celebrities being painfully ignored. So, right from the start, I dissociated myself from the 'celebrity' tag and tried to be as regular as possible. I wanted to be noticed for being me and not for what I did. I did not succeed in making other people see me like that but it did make things clear in my head.

When people complimented me for a job well done, I smiled and accepted it. When they said I did a bad job, I smiled (and silently disagreed). I am confident that they are wrong for one reason and one reason alone. Never in all my years of working before the camera have I given anything but hundred per cent of my effort. So when they said I didn't do a good job, to me it only meant they didn't like what I did.

> **Note to self:** If your best isn't good enough – that's just too bad. No point beating yourself up about it.

Since my fashion sense was non-existent in any case, I didn't draw too much attention when I went out. And the more normal I acted – 'so unlike a celebrity' – the more people seemed to like me. People have always had a different attitude towards me, especially after *Koffee with Anu*. People treated me like someone they knew. I would hear someone call out my name and would frantically try to put a name to the face when they would say, 'We love your show!' and I'd realize I didn't know them after all.

There were times when I wished they would maintain some distance. I recall how once I was sitting next to a co-star whom everyone spoke to in hushed tones as they got her autograph. One lady got an autograph from her, and then turned to me and pinched my cheek and said, 'You are just like my daughter!' I was startled. I wished they would treat me like they did my co-star. But now I realize what a compliment that was. I had been accepted as part of the family. To them I signified the girl next door who had succeeded in what they thought was a glamorous job.

My move to London signified the end of that phase. I was no longer in the public eye.

I came to England many years ago with such different plans, living someone else's dreams. But this time it was just for me and my happiness. It was surprising how easily I slipped into daily routines of trains and polite pleases and thank-you-very-much-indeeds. After a few days I even started developing a British accent. Of course, the British would be the first to protest that *they* are not the ones with an accent – it's like saying I have a Tamil accent when I speak Tamil. But you have to admit that there is something incredibly attractive about the way the British speak their language. And the various accents (despite British protests) are quite interesting.

The London accent is lazy and lethargic. Then there are those who chop off the t's – I think that's called Estuary English, where they say 'we ra' for 'wet rat' – and the Welsh accent, which sounds like a Bengali speaking in English. And, of course, scores of others that I am sure to come across in the future.

I thoroughly enjoyed walking along the streets of London, swathed in mismatched clothes and not being noticed. It is wonderful how disinterested they are when it comes to other people – and I mean this in an entirely positive sense. Especially when it comes to what women wear. I saw women displaying eye-popping amounts of cleavage (and the only eyes that were popping were mine!) and women with incredibly short skirts hurrying along in the cold and they didn't result in any raised eyebrows.

I suppose this is where the age-old debate between culture and modesty would pop up. Simply to amuse myself, I transposed (in my mind) these women onto the streets of Madras and I couldn't help chuckling at the reaction they would draw from men and women alike. It is curious, really. I am not a prude – well, not all the time – but sometimes I think I am too liberal to be completely accepted back home. At the same time, I feel I am too much of a prude in other places. I suppose what I'm saying is that I'm a misfit. Or else a chameleon who has her colour change out of sync!

As I went through busy train stations, I noticed I was the only one who was walking in a leisurely manner watching people. Everyone else was running for a train or running to work. It made for a pleasant change for me to be in a public place and remain completely anonymous. Don't get me wrong, it's not that I get mobbed back home. But it is not the same as being just another Indian woman in London.

As the days went by, I got used to not being recognized. And when it didn't happen on the streets, or in restaurants, or in malls and supermarkets, I started getting quite complacent.

That's when I had a bizarre accident at home. I ended up hitting my head on a cupboard, splitting the skin on my forehead and bleeding like a stuck pig! Graham rushed me to the A&E (accidents and emergency) in Lewisham. I walked in on my own steam (it was after all an itty bitty cut) with a white bath towel held to my forehead and was asked to wait. I watched a not quite mentally stable man having an argument with a not quite sober man with a not quite level-headed woman playing arbitrator. The receptionist caught my eye and cheerily said, 'Welcome to the real side of London.' I smiled at her weakly and settled down, trying to avoid eye contact with the weirdoes.

A few hours later I was called in to see the nurse and while she was examining me, the receptionist came running in all out of breath and said, 'Are you a faymus actress? Cos there'sh a goiy outsoide who saysh you ah!'

I love the accent lady, but so much for anonymity. I mean, of all the places to get recognized, it has to happen in the A&E in Lewisham where I am sitting holding a bath towel to my bleeding forehead! I spent the next few minutes trying to convince them that I was not all that famous but rather the kind of person who was somewhat known. They thought I was being modest. Obviously they hadn't heard of Kamal Haasan, Rajinikanth and other stars.

They were finally distracted when they noticed that my blood pressure was way off the charts. I knew it was only because the instrument was faulty because I could sense the systolic and diastolic reading when the darn thing was pumping and releasing pressure on the band. But they didn't know that and the reading was wild enough for them to think I was going to splatter open like a *dhrishti pooshinikka*. I was grateful for the distraction and encouraged them to take several more readings until they admitted that the instrument was faulty.

By then the 'faymus actress' story had taken a backseat and I was being examined for the cut on my forehead and pronounced fit enough to go back home. I walked out with the towel still clutched to my forehead and looked around the waiting area for the culprit who had blown my cover. There was this mousy guy huddling in the corner and I studiously ignored him as I sailed out of the emergency.

As I stepped out into the streets, the anonymity swamped me all over again and I felt comforted as I walked up to the parked car wearing scruffy pyjamas, a mismatched cardigan and a white bath towel held to my forehead for effect. (I must confess I milked the head injury story for all it was worth for the next few days.)

Note to self: You may be identified in the oddest of places – don't get too complacent in your anonymity and try to rob the bank!

A part of me resented the fact that I couldn't even have a cut on my forehead without having my so-called celeb status thrown at my face. Then again, I knew what I was getting into when I started work as an actress. So I shrugged the resentment away, tucked my hand into Graham's and walked gingerly to the car.

It had been more than three years since that incident. I was now on my way to becoming a resident.

As milestones go, it's no big deal but it *was* a big deal in one other way – January 2013 was the month that my 'spouse' visa expired and I had to make an application for it to be converted into an ILR (Indefinite Leave to Remain – in other words, a resident). I was told that it was a mere formality, as it was obvious that I was not a refugee who had married a white man in order to live on welfare in the UK.

But having been brought up in India, I always got nervous when I had to deal with government agencies. Plus I was worried about the surname. (My surname, while having positive connotations in Tamil Nadu, doesn't necessarily have the same connotations from an immigration point of view in the Western world and my dress code and backpack don't really dispel stereotypes.)

Much to Graham's amusement, I sat down months in advance to fill out the form and get the documents ready. As the day for the appointment approached, I spent hours labelling and filing the papers. Graham tried to tell me not to worry so much but my vivid imagination being what it is, I paid no heed to his reassurances. Instead I was making contingency plans. What if they threw me out of the country ... those kinds of contingency plans. Graham's assurance that my surname had nothing to do with the outcome fell on deaf ears.

On the day of the appointment I was less nervous than I had been on earlier occasions but I was still jittery. I checked the route to the office four times, wrote down directions and emailed myself the address. I checked, double-checked and triple-checked papers and took a deep breath and set out with Graham. Who, by the way, was far more interested in the book he was going to read while we waited at the Home Office.

We got there with plenty of time to spare and wandered aimlessly for a bit before we were allowed into the building. Prelim check done, payment made, case registered and biometric done in under an hour. Now it was a matter of waiting for the case to be considered and a decision to be made.

As I settled down in the waiting area, clamping down on

my nervousness, I heard a voice say, 'You are Anu Hashhan, isn't it?' I was so nervous I didn't bother correcting his pronunciation. I looked at the young boy sitting across from me and nodded my head. He was most excited. Could he have a photograph with me? I reminded him that this was the Home Office and owing to security reasons, photography was not allowed. I wasn't about to let him take a photo of us and have security haul us off unceremoniously from the premises. He looked downcast but brightened up when I agreed to give him an autograph. He took it from me and almost immediately was on the phone jabbering about how he had met Kamal Haasan's niece. The darn surname, hey?

As his voice faded into the haze of my nervous wait, I caught a movement in front of me from behind the glass partition where the immigration officers sat.

I looked up to see an officer beckoning me to come forward. My brain went into overdrive. There were 300-plus people waiting in the hall and this man was singling me out? What did it mean? Maybe I wasn't allowed to talk to the other applicants? Did the young boy yell my surname out too loudly?

I walked up to the counter and the officer smiled at me. 'Do you remember me?' he asked.

And I did. This was the same officer who had processed my spouse visa and he had spoken to me about Rajinikanth sir. I smiled in relief as I recalled our conversation which had started off when he noticed my surname. We chatted for a few seconds and then he thrust a paper through the window and asked me to autograph it. I did so in a daze and came back to settle down beside a very amused Graham.

Half an hour later, another summons and another nervous walk up to another counter. I got my papers back. All the officer said was, 'There you go.'

I paused and asked timidly, 'My ILR?'

He nodded and said, 'All done. Should reach you over the next week.'

I beamed at him and almost skipped back to Graham. He smiled at me indulgently and asked, 'Happy now?'

I grinned back and looped my arm through his. As I jauntily walked out of the Home Office I said, 'You're right ... my surname had nothing to do with it.'

'Typical that you should go for your residence permit and end up signing autographs at the Home Office, huh?' he teased. I was too happy and relieved to get embarrassed about that.

We reached home and I was in the kitchen making us a celebratory cup of coffee when Graham rushed in. He was yelling something and I couldn't make out what he was saying. I was about to panic when I saw the huge grin on his face and then his words registered: 'I saw you! I saw you!' He dragged me out of the kitchen to the telly, and there I was on British television in the Sky Movies commercial.

In a flash, I remembered being in a press conference a few years ago. One of the questions posed to me was: 'If you had not been a Hasan, do you think you would have succeeded?' Without even pausing, I remember replying, 'Yes,' and smiling as I waited for the next question. I think my conviction shone through, for the audience broke into spontaneous applause. But later the question nagged at me. Was that their image of me?

I was dragged back to the present with a jolt – the last shot was a tight close-up of me laughing at something ... my usual belly laugh.

This time I hopped up and down in excitement. After almost twenty years before the camera, for the first time I felt thrilled seeing my face on television. This, for me, was the symbol of a personal victory.

Note to self:
Starting from scratch after having succeeded elsewhere takes courage but the fruits of that particular labour can be the sweetest.

As I smiled happily at Graham, I realized he was right in more ways than one. I had done this purely on my own steam. My surname had nothing to do with it.

But when others look from the outside what do they see? How do I, myself, look at other people? I replay a scene from memory.

She submits herself to the boring process that is getting ready to look her best. Swipe, swipe, clean – a passing comment on how oily her skin is. The remark typical of make-up men who like to stoke the fires of insecurity. What he doesn't realize is that she is more comfortable in her skin than he thinks. She smiles vaguely and ignores him, her mind drifting away into the complications that are going to make the approaching days fairly interesting. She returns to reality with a start when her subconscious warns her that he is using too much foundation. She reminds him that her skin is thin and with too much foundation she's likely to end up with lines. He mumbles something about getting her skin to glow and continues to blend. She goes back to her thoughts.

He sticks a mirror before her and asks her to take a look. She thinks she looks a little brighter than she should, but the camera is unforgiving and she decides to concede that he knows his job. She makes the appropriate noises, knowing that even if she objects he isn't going to do a damn thing about it. He tells her he is going to start on her eyes and she feels a little nervous. She has noticed that he is a bit careless with the way he moves his hands and she is not looking forward to having him poke her eye accidentally.

She nervously allows him to proceed. He is blending eye-shadow on her eyelids. It is a ghastly shade of salmon. She is fairly certain that with her wheatish complexion she is going to look weird to put it mildly, but she has learnt enough in the past to know that it is prudent not to comment till the job is complete. So she holds back her words of reservation and waits for him to finish. Eyeliner, mascara, a small poke, an indrawn breath of pain, a hasty apology and the process is complete. She looks distractedly at her face as he finishes. It is the face of a stranger. She smiles and the familiar grin reassures her despite the salmon pink eye-shadow. She nods at him and says, 'Nice.' He is practically preening. He brings a strip of butter paper and proceeds to dab her face. She knows he is longing for her to ask him what he is doing. She obliges. 'German technology,' he says. 'Absorbs the oil from your skin.' Still stuck on that, are we? She lets it pass, not wanting to tell him we've been using butter paper for lining baking trays for who knows how long. How do you expect a make-up man to know about baking? German technology, indeed.

She walks into the sets and the cameraman smiles in welcome. The director looks at her face critically, her clothes. She is used to being examined in this way. The initial embarrassment has long since faded. Nowadays she joins them in their examination and adjusts and tucks and tugs and blends. She looks at her director, waiting for her to describe the shot. She has some trouble getting started. The man acting with her is nervous and tries to cover his nervousness by cracking inane jokes. The fact that she is calm seems to make him more nervous. Usually she takes an effort to calm her co-actors but today she doesn't have the energy and she quietly stands there, her hand resting on the refrigerator that is being used as a prop.

She hears the director saying 'Ready' and realizes that she is going to roll camera without even doing a rehearsal. She tells the director that it's better to do a dry run. She doesn't add that it might be necessary for the guy opposite her, even if not for herself. It's a fairly simple shot. She has to tug open the gift-wrapping on the refrigerator, open the door, look up at him and smile in surprise. All he has to do is stand and smile back at her. But amateur actors have been known to flub even that.

They do a dry run and fine-tune a few things. 'Don't look up at him until you see the gift inside,' her director says. She nods at the director and then withdraws into herself. She breaks down her actions into emotionless sequences – smile at him, look down at refrigerator, reach for the bow, tug it open, open the fridge, look at the gift inside, register it, change to surprise, look up at him with surprise, change it to delight and smile. Okay. Got that.

The director calls, 'Action'. Our actress flawlessly executes her sequence. The director is happy. She is ready for the next shot – a close-up. But they have to change the lighting. The director asks her to 'go relax' so she saunters back into the room and the make-up man bustles in after her. He is unhappy with the way her skin is – yes, you got it right – oily. Dab dab, blend. Oh look, your eyeliner is running. She can't resist telling him, I told you so. He does some repair work. They are ready for the next shot. She has to go back. She lazily listens to her directions and again executes with ease, the style and comfort exactly what the director wanted. She knows it's easy because when she is acting, she focuses only on that. Not on scheduling, absenteeism, new equipment, equipment hiring logistical issues or personal problems. Yes – she has a lot to worry and think about. She has now begun to use these shoots as an escape from the mundane tensions that have crept into her life. The complications that she creates – those that come her way – all of them recede into background noise. And she slips into her role, leaving them all behind. Yet she knows she returns to them. And when she returns, her oily skin, the few extra kilos, the dark circles under her eyes – all these recede into the background. She dons her real-life role with an ease that is essentially her again. She lives two lives – one where she solely uses her intelligence and the other where she uses her looks, skills as well as her intelligence. Both lives are mutually exclusive. One doesn't overlap into the other. And she can't imagine how it would be without one of these compartments.

A part of her notices that her face has become better with

the passage of time. There is more character now. Sadness adds to the appeal. She wonders why. She looks critically in the mirror. Age, experience, pain, wisdom, disappointment, understanding and acceptance – all blended into her salmon pink eyeshadow and she smiles. I smile back at my image of her.

CONCLUSION

As I finish writing this, I lean back on my chair and take a deep breath.

There – it's done. The book that I have always wanted to write. I hope that some of what I have written finds resonance within you. When I look back at my finished work, it brings to mind a picture of me taken during a recent college reunion. I am grinning widely but squinting at the camera – cross-eyed Mary, that's me.

I click on the link that takes me to the picture. It makes me smile. There I am, unfazed and unrepentant, my attitude to life out there in plain sight for all to see. That's what this book is too... You can see the lines, the experience, the self-deprecating tone and if you look hard enough, the blunted pain of hard lessons learnt. But you will still feel the happiness shining through and damned if it doesn't make you smile.

I look back at my life so far– it has not been perfectly lived but it has been perfect for me.

My parents equipped me well to face it and I owe them my gratitude. My mistakes have served me well. And my natural tendency to bob right back up to the surface has ensured that my life has almost always been... *Sunny Side Up.*

ACKNOWLEDGEMENTS

When it comes to acknowledgements do I acknowledge the people who have helped shape my book or those that have helped shape me? Both, I suppose.

I owe my thanks to my agent (and now friend) Priya Doraswamy at Lotus Lane Literary for believing in me (I am not sure what I enjoyed more – working with you or our crazy face-time calls!), and to Gandhi Kannadhasan for introducing us.

Some of these stories first appeared in *JFW*, south India's leading magazine for women. Thank you Bina Sujit – without you I would not have started that journey in the first place.

Thanks to Harper Collins for making this foray of mine an enjoyable one. Karthika, it has been a pleasure. Bidisha, my editor, you may disagree with the previous statement, but I promise to make it up to you with ice cream!

My friends Kripa, Ranga, Abe, Purni and Anantha – I love you.

Thank you, Joe Eshwar, for the wonderful picture.

Thanks to my long-suffering family – no, it is not over yet! Not by a long shot!